"*Diamonds, Pearls & Stones* is fresh and innovative in its ability to celebrate and address rites of passage and rituals for modern young women all over the world. Jennifer Read Hawthorne and Barbara Warren Holden share their gift of bridging diverse women worldwide, encouraging the female voice to soar, and compassionately inspiring women to tap into their own individual and unique essence."

Alyssa, age 28

"This book is positively inspiring for women of all ages—the best advice and guidance a woman can get in order to live a fulfilling, peaceful, harmonious life. If everyone in the world read this book, I believe this would be a Utopian society."

Jessica, age 23

"This book gives young women an intimate portrayal of the experiences and wisdom our elders have to offer, letting us know that we are not alone in our emotional, professional and love struggles. After reading this, I am more at peace with what it means to be a woman."

Mary, age 24

"It's nice to know that what's happening to me is universal!"

Gabrielle, age 18

"This is a book I will always keep around so I can reread the wisdom within it. It gives insights from a deeper level than most people are willing to go."

Amy, age 21

"The beautiful knowledge I have learned from these extraordinary women of the world has shown me who I really am and what I stand for. I have found the true meaning of my existence, and I thank you for that."

Asia, age 18

"This book has a lot of great advice for women my age. Some of these pieces of wisdom are priceless, and you can't get them from anyone except older women. The book is packed with role models, each of whom has a knowledgeable perspective that every young woman can take advantage of."

Kemen, age 19

Diamonds, Pearls & Stones

Jewels *of* Wisdom *for* Young Women *from* Extraordinary Women *of the* World

Jennifer Read Hawthorne and Barbara Warren Holden

Health Communications, Inc.
Deerfield Beach, Florida

www.hcibooks.com

Library of Congress CIP data is available from the Library of Congress.

ISBN 0-7573-0155-X

Publisher: Health Communications, Inc.
3201 S.W. 15th Street
Deerfield Beach, FL 33442-8190

Cover artwork by Mara Friedman
Cover design by Lawna Patterson Oldfield
Inside design by Shepley Hansen
Inside formatting by Dawn Von Strolley Grove

To our mothers, Maureen H. Read and Louise Warren,
our first and dearest mentors, with love and gratitude

CONTENTS

ACKNOWLEDGMENTS

Our deepest gratitude goes to the women who so graciously shared their thoughts, their hearts and their wisdom with us for this book. We continue to be deeply touched by your generosity and willingness to reveal your most intimate feelings and experiences to support young women.

To our publisher, Peter Vegso, and the entire team at Health Communications, Inc., especially our editor, Allison Janse, we say thank you for your love and support, and for "doing business differently."

Thanks also to our editors, Elinor Hall, Karla Christensen, Lilli Botchis and Paul Holden, for your insights, wisdom and knowledge—and your willingness to tell the truth.

To the young women who graciously read this book in advance and shared your feedback: Your insights made us laugh with joy and weep with gratitude for validating the value of this book. Thank you, Kemen Austin, Sherry Biskup, Asia Dianni, Mary Estrin, Amy Hawthorne, Morgan Lazarro-Smith, Masha Mikulinsky, Alyssa Miller, Gabrielle Read-Hess and Jessica Wald.

To Ginger Nelson, Martha Bright and Helen French, our deepest gratitude for the administrative support and counsel you so generously gave us.

To Mara Friedman, Shepley Hansen of Bluebird Graphics and the HCI Art Department, thank you for your exquisite contributions to our book's cover and design.

To our family and friends, we acknowledge that there are no greater blessings in our lives than you.

And finally, to the young women we interviewed in the course of creating this book, we thank you for telling us what you longed to know—and for reminding us of the deep joy and satisfaction that happen when we connect with each other generation to generation, woman to woman.

INTRODUCTION

I long to put the experience of fifty years at once into your young lives,
to give you at once the key to that treasure chamber,
every gem of which has cost me tears and struggles and prayer,
but you must work for these inward treasures yourselves.

—HARRIET BEECHER STOWE

From the beginning of humankind, the passing on of wisdom from the elders to the younger, less experienced members of the "tribe" has been an essential and natural part of the social well-being of all cultures. For women especially, circles around fire and hearth have provided a sense of belonging, as well as the opportunity for younger women to receive the insights, wisdom and support of older women to awaken their own truths and gifts.

But unfortunately, this natural flow of support and wisdom between the generations has been lost in our culture, replaced by mass media and technology, resulting in a generation longing for some sense of connectedness, purpose and truth. Many young people are floundering through their most vital years feeling isolated, unsure and unfulfilled. This book is the outpouring of our heartfelt recognition of this isolation and our desire to bridge this gap by presenting the experiences and accrued wisdom of some of today's most extraordinary, powerful and fulfilled women.

The title, *Diamonds, Pearls & Stones,* represents the struggles, prayers and victories that have cultured these pearls and fashioned these diamonds. It is also an offering of the stepping-stones—the ones upturned, the ones stumbled upon, the ones turned smooth by the tides of yearning for truth in these women's hearts and souls. It is the same yearning we all feel, a call for the deepest love that we instinctively know is possible for ourselves and for our world.

Diamonds, Pearls & Stones addresses the biggest issues young women told us they are facing today: self-acceptance, body image, emotions, sexuality, relationships, making choices, friendship and support, career and purpose. To these topics we have added what we feel are essential chapters on how to take care of ourselves as women and where authentic power for women lies. At the end of each chapter, we have included a section called Turning Your Own Stones, offering the reader questions to reflect on and possibly discuss with other women in groups or online chat rooms.

The contributors to this book include mostly women from ages 36 to 104. We met with them individually and in groups, we "talked" with them by phone, fax and e-mail, we found them in hundreds of books in libraries and bookstores. We unearthed and distilled pages and pages of exquisite stories, insights and memories, many of which brought us to tears. We discovered that the women sharing their life experiences were just as hungry to share their gifts as those eager to receive.

We also drew on the wisdom of a handful of younger women, wise beyond their years, who are either leaders or counselors for other young women. We researched from multiple sources celebrities and experts in different fields to fully complete the jewel box. And we even included a sprinkling of quotes from men who we felt had something relevant and rich to offer.

We feel it's important to recognize that the feminine lives within all of us. As our friend Carol Parker so beautifully said: *Female power is not gender specific; it's a particular voice. The power of the feminine can come through men or women. It's not mental, intellectual, rational or linear—it's spontaneous, heartfelt, light-filled clarity. It's like the call of wild geese flying overhead. What are they talking about? You can almost tell—they're joyful, they're alive, they're going home. They're just expressing pure life itself.*

We believe young women today are bright with an intelligence deeply based in an intuitive knowingness that will recognize and resonate with the truths within this book. Your journey belongs to you; we simply offer this book as a reminder that we are all going home together, an unbroken circle of women in support and gratitude for each other. You are not alone, and we deeply care.

Jennifer Read Hawthorne & Barbara Warren Holden

1

ACCEPTING YOURSELF

◆

The person you are trying to be
is probably not nearly as interesting
as the person you are.

—Masha Mikulinsky, student

CREATING *your own* REALITY

Life is not the way it's supposed to be. It's the way it is.
The way you deal with it is what makes the difference.

—VIRGINIA SATIR, FAMILY THERAPY PIONEER

- We create our own reality! Life is not something that just happens to us. If you believe that, you will always feel like a victim. You are responsible for the joy or the pain or the abundance in your life.

  —Elinor Hall, life skills coach

- There's a distinction between the *story* of what we think is going on and what's really happening. Most of what we think is reality is just interpretation. If we change what we think, we can fundamentally change reality.

  —Beth VanArsdale Krier, divorce attorney

- I think of life itself as a wonderful play that I've written for myself, and so my purpose is to have the utmost fun playing my part.

  —Shirley MacLaine, actress

- . . . The greater part of our happiness or misery depends on our dispositions and not on our circumstances.

  —Martha Washington, American First Lady

Start telling the truth about yourself. When you have a bad hair day, instead of saying "I'm ugly," try saying, "I'm having a bad hair day."

—J & B

BEING *who you* ARE

There is a vitality, a life force, an energy that is translated through you; and because there is only one of you in all of time, this expression is unique.

—MARTHA GRAHAM, DANCER & CHOREOGRAPHER

- Self-acceptance is not something you can get from anyone else; it can only come from you. It's not about liking yourself all the time—it means accepting yourself without conditions. It's accepting where you are now in the process of life, as you would accept the unfolding of a flower at each step. It's focusing on the beauty of each stage.

  —*Terra Rafael, midwife & Ayurvedic practitioner*

- I've learned that I'm not an accident, not here by mistake. I'm here and I have value. My value doesn't depend on what I do; I'm simply valuable because I am, and learning that has helped me be positive about myself. And since I believe this about myself, I believe it about others.

—Joan Lescinski, CSJ, Ph.D., president, Saint-Mary-of-the-Woods College

- When I am trusting and being myself as fully as possible, everything in my life reflects this by falling into place easily, often miraculously.

  —Shakti Gawain, author

- There's always someone to tell you you have to. *Wrong. Don't.* Rather, spend time finding out who you *really are*. Work on being more of *that*. [It's] a lot better than the futile "gotta change" treadmill, which never really ends.

  —Shirley Jones in SUCCESS SECRETS OF SUPER ACHIEVERS by Jim Stovall

Someone called my inspiration phone line and left this message: "SARK, I send you waking naps, where for brief periods of time, you can stop working on yourself, and simply luxuriate in where you are right now, just as you are."

—SARK, *SUCCULENT WILD WOMAN*

COMPARING *yourself to* OTHERS

Normal is not something to aspire to, it's something to get away from.

—JODIE FOSTER, FILM DIRECTOR & ACTRESS

- Stop comparing yourself to others! Comparing is the fastest way to self-destruction. You can spend your whole life trying to have the perfect body, the perfect face, the perfect hair, the perfect weight, the perfect clothes, the perfect way of being. Cues from society can be fun things to play with, but the map of how to get to who you are or who you want to be is not on the outside—it's on the inside.

  —Wendy Bramlett, yoga teacher & studio owner

- You never know what's going on behind people's closed doors. The friend I imagined as having the perfect life later compared notes with me, and I got to see how she had experienced the same kind of breakdowns and vulnerability I had. We had *both* imagined the other to be so much better off.

  —Alexis Mayne, president, natural cosmetics company

- I struggled with self-esteem longer than I needed to. After about thirty-six years of age I said, "That's it!" I'm not putting any more time, money, research, study into improving my self-esteem. I've given it twenty years of attention, and I am just going to live my life now without trying to fix it. I realize nobody's perfect, and it's a waste of time to compare myself to others.

—Yaniyah Pearson, youth leadership director

◆

What makes us different from one another
is so much less important than what makes us alike.

—OPRAH WINFREY, TELEVISION TALK SHOW HOST

LIVING *from the* INSIDE OUT

It is not easy to find happiness in ourselves,
and impossible to find it elsewhere.

—AGNES REPPLIER, AMERICAN ESSAYIST

- From the wise old pinnacle of my forty-nine years, I want to tell you that what you're looking for is already inside you. . . . You can't buy it, lease it, rent it, date it or apply for it. The best job in the world can't give it to you. Neither can success, or fame, or financial security. . . .

  —Anne Lamott, author, Berkeley graduation talk, May 2003

- From the time we are very young, we are taught to look outside ourselves for things to base our self-esteem on: relationships, possessions, jobs, titles, others' opinions, our bodies, etc. But all these things are external and constantly changing—so how can they be the basis for anything? True self-acceptance means finding the part of you that does not change—the part that is deeper than your body, deeper than your mind, deeper than your emotions.

—JRH

- I learned very early on in life to listen to the opinions, feelings, needs and desires of my parents—and everyone and everything but my own inner voice. There is nothing more painful and hopeless than living one's life from the outside in, according to external directives. But then, there's nothing so sweet as finally giving up this illusory quest and meeting the Wisdom that has always been here, waiting within.

—Wendy Grace Danner, metaphysical teacher & counselor

I *often wonder what it would be like not to have mirrors.*
To breathe and feel—and not look.

—KAT SHEA, MASSAGE THERAPIST & HOMEOPATH

DEALING *with* INADEQUACY

Our deepest fear is not that we are inadequate.
Our deepest fear is that we are powerful beyond measure.

—MARIANNE WILLIAMSON, *A RETURN TO LOVE*

- Men are taught to apologize for their weaknesses; women for their strengths.

  —Lois Wyse, advertising executive

- I didn't belong as a kid, and that always bothered me. If only I'd known that one day my differentness would be an asset, then my early life would have been much easier.

  —Bette Midler, actress

- Beginning when we are girls, most of us are taught to deflect praise. We apologize for our accomplishments. We try to level the field with our family and friends by downplaying our brilliance.

  —Oprah Winfrey, television talk show host

- Always do the best you can—and appreciate the fact that you've always done the best you could. As our singer/songwriter friend Jan Smith sings, "If I could do it, I would have done it by now."

  —J&B

- There is nothing to attain. You are everything, united with everything. Nothing is missing, no lack. You must know this truth.

  —Chalanda Sai Ma, humanitarian & spiritual teacher

♦

Oh, I'm so inadequate. And I love myself!

—MEG RYAN, ACTRESS

LIFE CYCLES

To everything there is a season, and a time to every purpose under the heaven.

—ECCLESIASTES III

- Drink fully of each stage of the life cycle (maiden, mother, crone). Ask yourself: "Can I be all that it's possible to be at this phase of my unfolding?" When you are complete and full at each point in the cycle, then you are available for the next. Sometimes there is mourning for what you are leaving behind, what is being lost, but it is ultimately a celebration of the richness of the ever-evolving nature of human life.

  —Melissa Michaels, educator, social artist & mother

- You're in a cycle of life where it's natural to be energetic, impulsive, exploring, seeking. So don't feel you should know all the answers and be established already in a state of acceptance and ease! If you're having self-esteem issues, you're right on target. It's what almost every young woman struggles with!

—Terra Rafael, midwife & Ayurvedic practitioner

- Experienced, creative women know that their creativity moves in cycles of birth, death and rebirth. Surrendering to the cycles instead of fighting with them is a skill of the creative warrior.

—Gail McMeekin, THE 12 SECRETS OF HIGHLY CREATIVE WOMEN

◆

The only thing you can be sure of in life is that everything changes.
Life is a dance of negative and positive, and one does not exist without the other.

—WENDY BRAMLETT, YOGA TEACHER & STUDIO OWNER

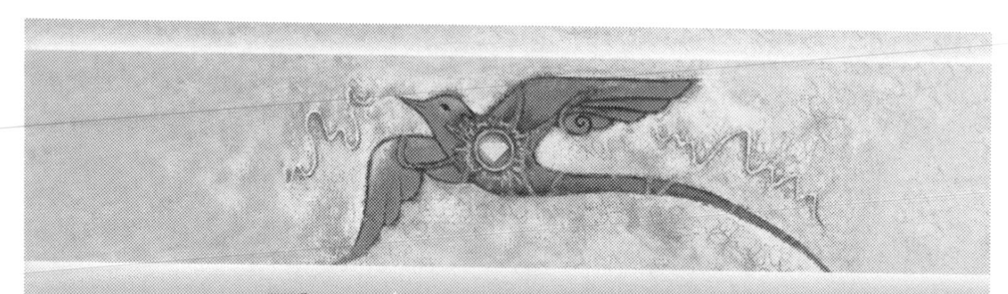

The DIAMOND MINE:
What is your greatest gift you bring to the world?

- Empathy—the gift of relating with everybody. It grows as I grow older, being able to put myself in other people's shoes. I'm constantly connecting with everyone—the cashier, the waiter, the man I buy my water from, the woman I buy my wheat grass trays from, the person sitting next to me on the subway listening to Mary J. Blige—even with their earphones on I can hear it and start grooving with them.

  —Jennifer Claire Moyer, actress

- My greatest gift is my connection to the earth. In our culture we've lost our connection to the earth, our mother, and the result is anxiety and depression. I take people on vision quests and retreats in the wilderness because that is my passion. I'm a bridge between people and the natural world.

  —Carol Parker, psychotherapist & wilderness guide

- I can make things happen. If someone has an idea, I can come up with ten ways to approach it and make it happen on the material level. When I was about four years old, my father said I should go into advertising because I had so many ideas. "What's an idea?" I said. But by the time I got to college, I studied public relations and found fascinating work in special events and publicity.

—Arielle Ford, media relations expert & author

- My life is about healing. Even when I'm not working, this gift comes through. When I had a near-death experience as the result of a horse accident, I became immersed in immense light. Veils hiding truth were lifted, and a great capacity to heal resulted from this. It's like being a big bonfire: whoever gets close gets warm. I don't have to do anything but be myself.

—Kiki Corbin, naturopathic doctor & minister

- My greatest gift is my unfailing commitment to nurture a vision of a different and better world. Every day when I wake up it makes sense to me for the world to live cooperatively. My gift is to hold that vision for the world—in my conversations with others, in the way I vote, in the way I march for peace, choose to shop, write my congressman, and the degree to which I get involved in local environmental and national political issues.

—Candace Freeland, photographer, musician & peace activist

- To be able to share love. This manifests itself in numerous ways: hugging people after our concerts or even something as simple as tidying up a room—making the world more beautiful through joy and love. I also feel that when singing and chanting I can caress the essential being of everyone present, not only through my voice, but also through my eyes. I used to sing with my eyes closed, until I realized this. Since then, I've become more conscious of opening my eyes when I sing.

  —Deva Premal, singer & musician

- I was on the streets at the age of fourteen. I had some pretty tough times, but the result was that I have a natural ability to see both sides of a situation and not judge others. I have cultured a great deal of compassion and sense of fairness by putting myself in others' positions and seeing through their eyes. I think going through tough things makes you not only stronger, but cultures character and compassion for others.

  —Jenn Holden, social worker

- If I have a gift, it's about creating, renovating, forming, building, generating, rehabbing, realtering, remaking, refabricating. Simply, it's about making things, whether a Karo pecan pie or a barn in my backyard. As someone once said, "What is a life if not a chance to make something from nothing?"

  —Pamela George, Ph.D., professor & painter

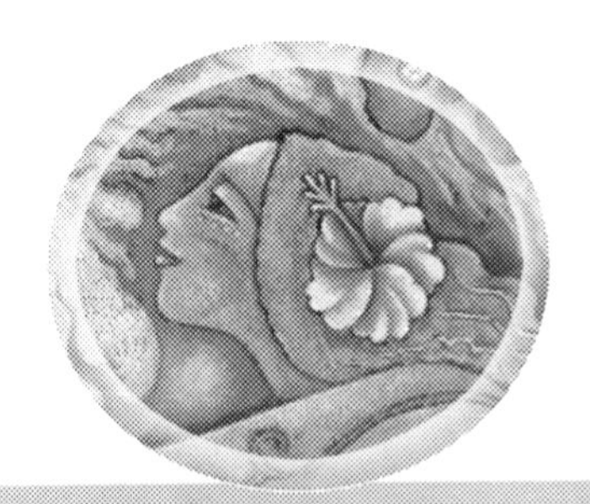

STEPPING-STONES *for* ACCEPTING YOURSELF

- We waste so much time complaining about things we can't change. If it's not in your control, either let it go or find a creative way to deal with it.

  —J&B

- Creative expression is the gateway to self-acceptance. By that I mean facing issues of self-acceptance openly in creative ways, such as writing, drawing and performing.

  —Sage Hamilton, community leader & women's group facilitator

- I couldn't remember a lot about my childhood, so I asked my parents to tell me what I was like when I was young. I loved listening to their beautiful memories of me, again and again, like a favorite bedtime story, helping me to heal by filling in the gaps of a troubled childhood with sweetness.

—Becca Ferry, sacred arts painter & collector

- When I was twenty-five I started getting individual and group therapy. It made me realize why I was the way I was, what prompted me to do things and what I was not happy about in my life. It was a complete turnaround for me, and even today, it gives me a structure for figuring out what's going on with me.

  —Marsha Wright, marketing account executive

- I was a modern dancer at the age of eighteen. I used my body as a vehicle for knowing myself, because focusing on my body allows me to be totally present. In being totally present we can find acceptance of ourselves. It doesn't have to be dance—it can be walking, yoga, anything that allows you to go deeply into your own experience.

  —Dawn Hunter, organic gardener, dancer & fiber artisan

TURNING *your own* STONES

Get together with some girlfriends—in person or on-line—and ask yourselves these questions. You might want to write down the answers first, then share them with each other.

1. What is the "story" you are telling yourself about what is happening in your life? What is the reality?

2. What are some tools you've used to get to know yourself more deeply that you could share with others?

3. What excites you about the phase of life you are in?

4. What is the greatest gift you bring to the world?

2

Living in Your Body

◆

If you don't take care of your body,
where will you live?

—Rosie Estrin, healer & counselor

FEELING VITAL *and* ALIVE

Vitality! That's the pursuit of life, isn't it?

—KATHARINE HEPBURN, ACTRESS

- Start from the inside. Whatever makes you feel vital, strong, free, balanced and beautiful—make that your priority. Then the body will line up with that. Rather than trying to make the body beautiful, it will be the by-product of feeling really good.

  —BWH

- I am always amazed at how wonderful men and women look when they are comfortable in their bodies, regardless of the shape or size, and how even the most classically beautiful people appear unattractive when they are constricting [their bodies].

  —Donna Farhi, The Breathing Book

- If we can just enjoy what we do and not be so concerned with how we look doing it, then we can allow the juice of life to move more freely through us. There is nothing wrong with looking good—that's part of the fun of being a woman—but looking good comes from feeling the beauty within. The sexiest women I've seen are the ones who are comfortable and confident, feeling into the depths of pleasure.

  —Alexis Mayne, president, natural cosmetics company

- I went through a phase where I saw skinny and long-limbed as beautiful, especially because I was a ballet dancer. After struggling with my health for about eight years, though, the concept of beauty has become linked almost completely with vitality, strength and fertility, and has almost nothing to do with the models that our society and media give us.

  —Morgan Lazzaro-Smith, youth mentor

◆

It's not normal to be hunched over and decrepit when old. Start now to discover what makes you feel alive—and you will always be beautiful, inside and out!

—ELINOR HALL, LIFE SKILLS COACH

LISTENING *to your* BODY

The body is always talking to us, if we only take the time to listen.

—LOUISE HAY, AUTHOR

- It's important to rest and move and play and exercise, but not the "should" kind—that constricts energy in every cell! Listen to your body; it naturally loves to express.

  —Tamara Matthews, therapist

- Our bodies tell us what's happening inside. When we smoke, take drugs, overeat or expose ourselves to too much stress, eventually, our bodies speak to us. When we don't feel well, there's a reason.

  —Kay Newton, hotel sales & marketing director

- Because we are fluid beings, we are easily influenced by our external environment. When we listen to our internal environment, the rhythms of the body, the breath and heart beat, we return to our own aliveness. This listening aligns us to a pace that is optimally vibrant, centered and healthy. Then we are less inclined to be affected by less authentic influences.

—Mary Capone, author, sound & movement teacher

- When we walk across the floor and stub a toe, our conditioning is to send hatred into the pain, to loathe it and really to try to put it out of our world—just the opposite of what it is calling out for. It is calling out to be held, to be cradled, to be accepted, to be touched with mercy, and to be explored.

  —Stephen Levine in TYING ROCKS TO CLOUDS, William Elliott

◆

Your body speaks in plain language: I'm hungry, I'm thirsty, I'm tired, I'm stressed . . . *Listening to it means hearing what it has to say, then treating it like your dearest friend.*

—J&B

I was a hard-core athlete and was so focused on what I wanted my body to *do,* that I didn't listen to it. I was so distracted that I didn't even realize I had a tumor growing in my head! After extensive surgery, I was forced to listen. That listening allowed me to heal more quickly and come out stronger in body and spirit.

—Mitzi Nicoletti,
massage therapist & health-care practitioner

THE MIND/BODY/SPIRIT CONNECTION

There is a fountain of youth: it is your mind, your talents,
the creativity you bring into your life and the lives of people you love.
When you learn to tap this source, you will have truly defeated age.

—SOPHIA LOREN, ACTRESS

- Bodies don't think, care, or have any problem with themselves. They never beat themselves up or shame themselves. They simply try to keep themselves balanced and to heal themselves. The body is never our problem. Our problem is always a thought that we innocently believe.

  —Byron Katie, LOVING WHAT IS

- There is an intelligence within the body that responds to whatever thoughts and attitudes we have, whether these are spoken or held silently within. It is important to love the body and to thank it for being. When treated with respect, the body responds accordingly.

  —Barbara Woolley, spiritual counselor, social worker & author

- The first level of taking care of the body comes from the intellect: For example, I can decide to go to bed earlier, to eat better or to take a walk every day. But real nourishment comes from accepting the body at the deepest level of the heart.

—Amsheva Mallani, healer & teacher

◆

The body, like everything else in life,
is a mirror of our inner thoughts and beliefs.

—LOUISE HAY, AUTHOR

CARING *for the* TEMPLE

I am a work of art. I am a miracle. My body is a temple that houses my spirit. Keep the house clean, keep the light burning, keep the heat on, keep the windows clear and open for the air to sweep through the spaces, keep the love flowing and keep the structure in good repair so you can Dance, Dance, Dance!

—VERA BERV, YOGA TEACHER

- What does the body really stand for? It houses our ability to experience happiness, and is a vehicle to take us towards fulfillment in life on all levels—emotional, mental and spiritual. Just as we care for our vehicles so that they will get us where we're going, so must we attend to our bodies.

  —Helena Meyer, cosmetician

- Keep your body strong and fit—it doesn't take much. Feel it, feed it and treat it like you love it. You'll come to love it if you treat it that way.

  —Diana Wald, artist & general contractor

- At some point I realized that I should be immensely grateful for having a human body, because of the potential it offers for evolutionary growth. And when I began looking at my body lovingly, as the instrument through which I could experience and express divinity, then everything changed in my relationship with my body.

  —Amsheva Mallani, healer & teacher

◆

There is no building made by human hands,
not even the Taj Mahal, that can compare to the marvel of a human body.

—MARIE-HELENE TOURENNE, FABRIC DESIGNER & MOTHER

SEXUALITY & SENSUALITY

Sex is hardly ever just about sex.

—SHIRLEY MACLAINE, ACTRESS

- Whatever you do, if you're feeling unloved or not getting enough attention, don't look to sex to take care of your frustration. Sex is very powerful, but it's no substitute for the open expression of your needs and concerns.

  —Judith Sherven, Ph.D., and James Sniechowski, Ph.D., THE NEW INTIMACY

- Sexuality is not always about partners and orgasms. It is also about how we live in our bodies. It is about being alive in our senses, yet not being controlled by them. It is about taking pleasure in stroking velvet, smelling bread baking, walking barefoot in the sand and gazing with wonder at a beautiful sunset. The paradox for women is that what we are told makes our body look sexy—high heels, flat bellies, makeup, tight skirts and a passive demeanor—are, in fact, the opposite of what makes us feel alive in our bodies. Sex without sensuality is a dry, mechanical experience.

—Charlotte Davis Kael, Ph.D., Women, Sex and Addiction

- Young women of this generation are struggling to decide whether to be sexual or not. I often ask my female clients to find their connection with their own sexuality—not the sex they have with their partners, but the place in them that holds this sexual energy. . . . It is possible to reclaim our bodies and our sexuality as something inherently sacred and as a direct link to the divine.

  —Wind Hughes, Daughters of the Moon, Sisters of the Sun

- Sexuality is all love; it's complete. Whether it's male to female, woman to woman or man to man, it's really ultimately human to human, soul to soul, essence to essence, love to love.

  —Lilli Botchis, Ph.D., alchemical researcher & adviser

- Sensuality does not wear a watch but she always gets to the essential places on time. She is adventurous, and not particularly quiet. She was reprimanded in grade school because she couldn't sit still all day long. She needs to move. She thinks with her body. . . .

  —Ruth Gendler, The Book of Qualities, in Changing Woman, Changing Work, Nina Boyd Krebs

- When I was younger, because of the celibate lifestyle I chose, I was not in a sexual relationship, but like any young person, I worried about what I looked like. Now I'm much more comfortable with myself as a sexual being and woman. I feel more vibrant and more self-confident about my body and myself. Sexuality is really energy for life. That's what I've come to understand about myself as a woman and a sexual being. I am a sexual being who has "energy for life."

  —Joan Lescinski, CSJ, Ph.D., president, Saint-Mary-of-the-Woods College

- Sexuality is the best thing about having a body. What's nice about having a long-term relationship is that you can deepen and develop your sexuality. But if you have a big plan about how it has to be, you will be disappointing yourself. There are no rules on timing, so you have to listen and trust yourself. Everyone is unique. It is like fruit ripening at its own pace.

  —Shar Lee, yoga teacher & cranial therapist

For women, sexuality and sensuality are corners of a triangle, at the pinnacle of which is the heart.

—J & B

ADVERTISING & *the* MEDIA

The beauty business is a $160 billion-a-year global industry, encompassing makeup, skin and hair care, fragrances, cosmetic surgery, health clubs and diet pills. Americans spend more each year on beauty than they do on education.

—*THE ECONOMIST*, MAY 24, 2003

- Keep the media out of your world as much as possible. It tries to shape your self-identity. The advertising industry is earning millions making you think you're not good enough, smart enough, sexy enough, small enough. Young people are their bait. You live your youth based on false data and then spend the rest of your life trying to unravel those beliefs.

  —*Stacey Hurlin, artist & community leader*

- Most popular women's magazines engender self-hatred. We must be aware that the images of "perfection" being sold to us are not real. The women in these magazines that we judge ourselves against have been physically altered—by doctors, by stylists, by photographic techniques. Their "perfection" is illusory, a marketing tool aimed at our insecurities. Why would we ever want to compare ourselves to an illusion?

—Andrea Girman, women's health practitioner & pediatrician

- We are bombarded with the propaganda of the body beautiful (most models are thinner than 95 percent of the female population), believing that what we see is normal and that we, in comparison, fall horribly short of these standards. We are willing to walk around in a state of semi-asphyxiation, holding our bellies in with belts, zippers and clothes two sizes too small, in order to cast the illusion of being youthful and fit. It is not necessary to feel bad to look good. We may, however, have to change the definition of what "looking good" means!

—Donna Farhi, The Breathing Book

◆

When we give our power to the media, we starve not only our bodies, but our hearts and souls as well.

—J & B

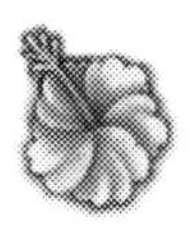

ADDICTIONS

You are not making changes because you are a bad person and you are doing it wrong. You make changes because you love yourself and you want to improve the quality of your life.

—LOUISE HAY, AUTHOR

- The most difficult things about addictions is acknowledging that you have them and finding the right people for support. The wrong people are those with like behavior. Finding a support group and mentors who are professionals at dealing with your form of addiction is a powerful step toward recovery.

  —*Marlena Long, M.D.*

- Native people can tell us a lot about the genocide caused by drugs, cigarettes and alcohol. In Western culture, we seem reluctant to admit that addiction is a major societal issue. Of course, denial is a major cornerstone of the disease. Native people are outspoken and clear about the effect of addiction—not only on individuals but on the entire culture.

—*Anne Wilson Schaef,* NATIVE WISDOM FOR WHITE MINDS

- When being in love means being in pain we are loving too much. When most of our conversations with intimate friends are about him, his problems, his thoughts, his feelings—and nearly all our sentences begin with "He . . .", we are loving too much . . . our loving itself becomes an addiction.

—*Robin Norwood,* WOMEN WHO LOVE TOO MUCH

- Recovery is a journey to the core of your being. It means turning inward and embracing all that you are, the light side and the shadow side, and being guided from the center of your being. It may mean casting out beliefs you learned in school, in church or at home. It means being true to yourself, even when it may create havoc. . . .

—*Charlotte Davis Kael, Ph.D.,* WOMEN, SEX AND ADDICTION

◈

Life itself is the proper binge.

—JULIA CHILD, WRITER & CHEF

WHAT *are you* HUNGRY FOR?

It seems to me we can never give up longing and wishing
while we are alive. There are certain things we feel
to be beautiful and good, and we must hunger for them.
—GEORGE ELIOT (MARY ANN EVANS), ENGLISH WRITER

- When you don't eat what your body is telling you it needs, your hunger doesn't get satisfied.

  —*Lynn Ginsburg & Mary Taylor, What are You Hungry For?*

- In my thirties, I noticed the trap of using food as a replacement for a more fundamental hunger. To heal this pattern, I began to explore the feelings driving it. Find support and cultivate tools to connect with the emotions that are calling out to be heard or fed within yourself. We are all hungry for the same thing—for intimate connection with spirit, with ourselves, with others—and it is nothing to be ashamed of. In fact, it's what we're here for.

—Andrea Girman, women's health practitioner & pediatrician

- I come from an Italian family and have a lot of joy around food. I also had a lot of angst around it earlier in life, but it is the joy that has remained. Food is a celebration, even if you're eating alone. Set up a beautiful table and make a luscious meal. It's not the food that's the problem; it's the attitude. When you deprive yourself of the joy, then you are starving yourself from what you really are longing for. The body knows exactly what it needs. Trust these impulses and get out of the mind, the rules and the struggle. When you give your body the message you care, it will respond in kind.

  —Mary Capone, author, sound & movement teacher

◆

Your soul is hungry for moist, rich communion.

—ROB BREZSNY IN *THE BODACIOUS BOOK OF SUCCULENCE*, SARK

MENSTRUATION & CYCLES

Women today are separate from the rhythms of nature more than any other time in recorded history. We have our monthly menstrual cycles to show us the way. Far from being a "curse," menstruation can be a quiet, reflective period—a time for each woman to honor the miracle of her body's potential for renewal.

—JUDITH LASATER, *RELAX AND RENEW*

- It's ironic we call it a period when it has nothing to do with a period. It's a cycle, more like a spiral than a stop! During my cycle I am more sensitive, emotional, inward, and in touch with myself and the psychic realms. I rest more and eat foods that are easier to digest. I alert people to treat me more tenderly during that time. If I get angry or frustrated during or after my cycle, it is usually because I didn't get what I needed during that time. I feel happier and healthier when I honor myself by responding to what I need.

—Terra Rafael, midwife & Ayurvedic practitioner

- Women are meant to feel deeply during our periods, and that is why we cry. This release is essential for our well-being, but our culture doesn't support us taking time off. I'd like to see women have the freedom to experience their cyclic lives as they did in ancient cultures, where women were closer to nature and took this time to rest and get more in touch with themselves. A period is a time of power and insight.

—Farida Sharan, natural physician

◆

There is no "one-fits-all" way to care for yourself during your period. But if there were, it would be to welcome it, appreciate it and listen to what you really need. Distracting yourself from your experience or imposing some rigid rules are distractions from your deepest feminine truth.

—BWH

BREASTS

Breasts in whatever shape or size are natural expressions of the heart—
the heart's outpouring from the mother in us all.

—TAMARA MATTHEWS, THERAPIST

- This culture is obsessed with large breasts and perfect bodies. While visiting the French side of St. Martin, where nude beaches are the norm, I was inspired by two old grandmothers in bikinis with their breasts hanging to their bellies. They seemed to feel no inhibition or shame but rather complete naturalness and acceptance. This is feminine beauty. Surround yourself with people who accept and enjoy their bodies as they are, and who support you in accepting and enjoying your body as it is.

  —Andrea Girman, women's health practitioner & pediatrician

- You don't have to like them, but you do have to love them. For me, breasts are about nourishing and sustaining, and also about sexuality and sensuality.

The best way to learn about your breasts and keep them healthy is to touch them, noticing what is normal and what is a change.

—Terra Rafael, midwife & Ayurvedic practitioner

- Cosmetic surgery is a major procedure. For breast augmentation you undergo anesthesia with a tube down your throat, and your skin is deeply cut into. It is not a gentle or benign process. It is worth it? If this is your choice, do it consciously and understand your motives. It is not a trivial procedure and recovery and possible side effects are significant. Ask yourself what it really means to be a woman.

  —Andrea Girman, women's health practitioner & pediatrician

- I have large breasts and they have been an issue for me as a dancer. I seriously considered getting a breast reduction. But I was working at a medical clinic in the seventies when a patient who was recovering from a reduction came in. Seeing her scars and stitches cured me from ever wanting to undergo such surgery. I chose to learn to love the healthy body I was born with. Making peace with ourselves as we are is one of the best gifts we can give ourselves.

  —Jan Kleinborg, women's health practitioner & nurse

◈

If someone doesn't like you because you have the wrong breasts, you're with the wrong person!

—J & B

AGING

We are always the same age inside.

—GERTRUDE STEIN, AMERICAN WRITER

- No matter what kind of body you've got, it won't be like that in twenty years. So how do you want to be when you're fifty? Live it now. Be wise, be loving, be caring about each other. Don't be afraid to open your heart. I'd rather have a broken heart every day of my life than to be shut down.

  —Rosie Estrin, healer & counselor

- The person who has a permanently scowling face did not produce that by having joyous, loving thoughts. Older people's faces and bodies show so clearly a lifetime of thinking patterns. How will you look when you are elderly?

  —Louise Hay, author

- We women take better care of others than ourselves. We struggle with self-care. If we can learn to accept and nourish our own bodies when we are young, we will have an easier time embracing growing older.

  —Tamara Matthews, therapist

- Enjoy your youth but understand that your body isn't always going to be so forgiving and resilient. Respect and nurture it so that it stays strong and healthy as long as possible. When you're young you have a lot of energy and passion to go for what you want and to accomplish things. Understand that this is a unique phase of life. I wish that I had known that and taken advantage of it.

  —Terra Rafael, midwife & Ayurvedic practitioner

◈

Nature gives you the face you have at twenty;
it is up to you to merit the face you have at fifty.

—COCO CHANEL, FRENCH COUTURIER

CULTURAL PERSPECTIVE

Women should travel around the world to realize that it's the U.S. that has a hang-up about bodies. The rest of the world does not demand a certain size and shape.

—STACEY HURLIN, ARTIST & COMMUNITY LEADER

- I like to remind myself that bodies naturally come in all shapes and sizes, because we all have a uniquely blended ethnic background. The part of the world that our ancestors came from determined what form their bodies took, as they evolved with an incredible wisdom to meet the demands of their particular environment.

  —Morgan Lazzaro-Smith, youth mentor

- I have gained twenty-five pounds in the last ten years. Would I like to lose some of that? Yes, probably. But as I've gotten rounder, I've also gotten softer. My emotions have gotten softer, and I've gotten more kind. My opinions, perspectives and judgments have all gotten softer. I have more acceptance of those around me as well as more self-acceptance. If you go to any other cultures—the South Pacific, Asia, Africa, the Mediterranean—women are naturally rounder and softer.

—Stacey Hurlin, artist & community leader

- "Beauty" has always been determined by culture and time. In the Renaissance, for example, the ideal of beauty was for women to be much heavier. Today's women would have been looked at as skeletal, not fetching at all . . . skinny giantesses with frightening faces!

—Shane Orne, riding coach & mother

◆

The Hawaiians taught me a lot about bodies; they see the body as the housing for the soul. We hear it, but we don't live it. We are always saying, "If I were thinner, if I were stronger or bigger, if I had curly or straight hair, things would be better."

—SHAR LEE, YOGA TEACHER & CRANIAL THERAPIST

TRUE BEAUTY

Beauty to me is being comfortable in your own skin.

—GWYNETH PALTROW, ACTRESS

- For most women, who we are is how big our breasts or hips are. But of course, our true beauty is the unseen body. It's the softness, the kindness, the gentleness, the femininity, the grace, the charm. You take the most beautiful actress or woman, and who is it that people really love? The one with the biggest heart.

  —Wanda Roth, fashion & jewelry consultant

- I was always looking for my beauty through someone else's eyes. When I was younger, I knew how to look "hot." After marriage, I wanted my husband to see me as beautiful. Now, I want to see my beauty through my own eyes.

  —Rae Bales, poet, writer & teacher

- Beauty is an internal light, a spiritual radiance that all women have but which most women hide, consciously denying its existence. What we do not claim remains invisible. *—Marianne Williamson, A Woman's Worth*

- Have you ever caught yourself in the mirror laughing? That's what it's all about. Laughing and catching yourself. Laughing at yourself, letting yourself go. It is when I feel the most beautiful, the most free to be myself.

  —Louise Warren, former actress & great-grandmother

- When I find myself obsessing on outer beauty, it's a great barometer to gauge how far out of myself I've strayed. Then I know it's time to attend to my inner world, time to listen and find the inner beauty.

  —Jenny Caroff, student

◆

We are changing the self-consciousness of a spotlight
on *the body for the self-consciousness of a light radiating* from *the body.*

—GLORIA STEINEM, AUTHOR & FEMINIST MOVEMENT LEADER

The DIAMOND MINE:
How do you get grounded?

- Being ungrounded—which is the best way for me to talk about this—means that I first notice the symptoms. I'm in my head—fearful, worried, chaotic or anxious. So I visualize my spine as a tree rooting down into the earth, until I feel connected with the earth. Then I find the symptoms disappear.

  —Becca Ferry, sacred arts painter & collector

- I'm just physical, very kinesthetic. You put your hand in water and just observe a stream moving—and you are there! You are the thing, you become it, just by bringing all of your awareness to that living entity. Going into something physical allows you to be filled up with wonder and awe—you're transported to a different way of perceiving.

  —Dawn Hunter, organic gardener, dancer & fiber artisan

- I eat well to get grounded. I'm learning that food that is vital and alive has some intelligence in it—and that seems to feed me at a deep cellular level. My body is responding very well, because it's getting the message that I'm finally putting food into it that's nurturing and loving for it.

  —Jacquelina Davis, LMT & NIA instructor

- Being ungrounded stems from the mind. Whenever I find myself starting to get in my head, I consciously take a breath through my nose, and let out a sigh. It's like slipping into a hot bath.

  —DH, business & family manager

- I've always been a person who knew how to get connected to the earth and feel good. But with four small children I couldn't go into my bedroom and meditate or do an hour and a half of yoga. Sun salutations (a series of yoga postures) are huge in my life. I begin every day with them and I do them again as the sun goes down. It takes six minutes to do six of them. They stretch every muscle in my body and they make me breathe.

  —Sue Huggins, full-time mother

- First, I like to do a long meditation followed by a good hike in the mountains in the high country—completely alone. Next, I love having a spa day with my partner. We create a spa atmosphere in our home or go to a hot springs and rent a room. Then we do it all—mud, massage, music, hot water, energy healing, and some sacred love and sexuality.

—Shari Hindman, healer, mother & businesswoman

- I become grounded through prayer, meditation and reflection. Second, I've been an organic vegetable gardener for thirty-five years. Contact with nature is extremely grounding, peace-inducing and bigger than myself. Third, through loving interactions with people I care about and who care about me . . . the friends and family of my life.

  —Joan Lescinski, CSJ, Ph.D., president, Saint-Mary-of-the-Woods College

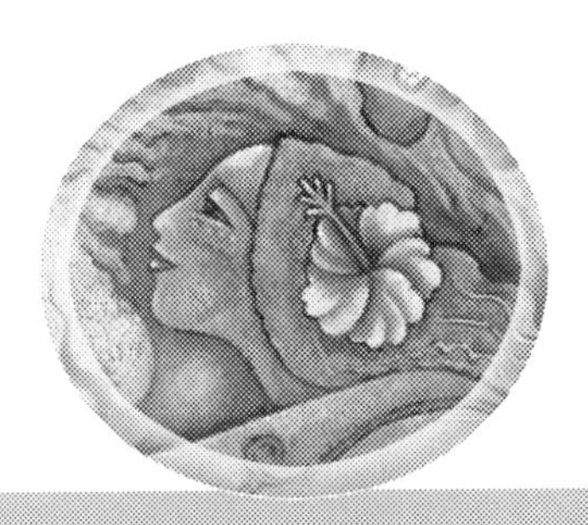

STEPPING-STONES *for* LIVING *in your* BODY

- EXERCISE. It's the most important thing in my life. Without it, I'm cranky, irritable, moody and tired. I'd drop it in a second if someone in my family had an emergency, but I do whatever I can to fit it in—even if it means we have to go out to eat.

  —Marsha Wright, marketing account executive

- SELF-MASSAGE. One of the ways we can know ourselves is through the pulsations and movements and rhythms of our bodies . . . our breath, our hearts, the involuntary muscles that are in constant motion . . . self-massage puts us more in touch with our bodies.

  —Jacquelina Davis, LMT & NIA instructor

- NATURE. Let the body move and be in nature. There's some kind of magic when you're out in nature that allows you to feel good about your body. It's a flow of energy that comes from the earth. It's so accepting—there's no judgment there. On some level that impacts us—it slips in past the intellect and informs the heart.

—Dawn Hunter, organic gardener, dancer & fiber artisan

- BREATH. Learn what the potential of the breath is. You can take little shallow breaths your whole life, but if you want to thrive, learn how to use your breath to open up your energy. More energy allows you to find the strength and openness that let you engage with the world more fully—and experience the more ecstatic realms of existence.

—Sue Berkey, yoga teacher & mother

- ADORNING. I love wearing soft flowing garments so they can accommodate my body as it changes even throughout the day. I like dressing up and makeup. We loved that as little girls—why not now? Loving your body means the feeding of it, the exercising it, the bathing, the dancing, the adorning, the feel of your own sensuality.

—Farida Sharan, natural physician

- Yoga. We started doing yoga about forty years ago, but don't think we didn't get exercise before that. We were younger and lived in New York City, we'd walk for miles because we couldn't afford to take the trolley. That was mighty good exercise. You don't have to get down on the floor to do yoga. You can get exercise from doing housework, gardening, all kinds of things—anything's better than sitting on your behind all day long.

—Sadie and Bessie Delaney, at ages 102 & 104,
The Delaney Sisters' Book of Everyday Wisdom

- Naps. Naps are the adult version of a child's fort.

—SARK, author

- Self-Examination. The more you know about your own body, the more empowered you are to care for it, enjoy it and heal it when there is an imbalance. Get a sense of what you look and feel like inside through self-exploration and anatomy diagrams. When you go for your next gynecological exam, ask your practitioner for a hand mirror so that you, too, can view yourself internally.

—Jan Kleinborg, women's health practitioner & nurse

- Loose Clothing. I see the breasts as extensions of the heart, the nurturing, flowing part of the heart. I advise young women to not wear bras all the time, to let yourself feel your clothing touch your skin and not be bound. It restricts the lymphatic system and is linked to health problems later in life. My advice is to air them more, enjoy and appreciate them more as the soft radiant expressions of your heart regardless of shape, size or sensitivity.

—Maurieke Shyelle, M.D. & women's health practitioner

- Listening. For a long time I had intense cravings for sugar and crunchy textures. I realized a lot of that was from anger held in my jaw; crunching hard foods helped release it a bit. I also felt a yearning for sweetness that was lacking in my life, and sugar was a boost for the fatigue I was denying. As I healed emotionally, these needs for external fulfillment dwindled. I employed various therapies and used the technique of asking my body directly what it wanted to tell me by directing my awareness to where I felt the craving.

—Susan Joy Schleef, belly dance instructor & data base administrator

- Cooking. I love cooking for people. But when I'm by myself, I cook myself the most beautiful, sensual, custom-made meals. I make the plate a work of art. It's a way to give myself what I love to give others, and a total indulgence in self-love. I find there's no more fulfilling food than that.

—BWH

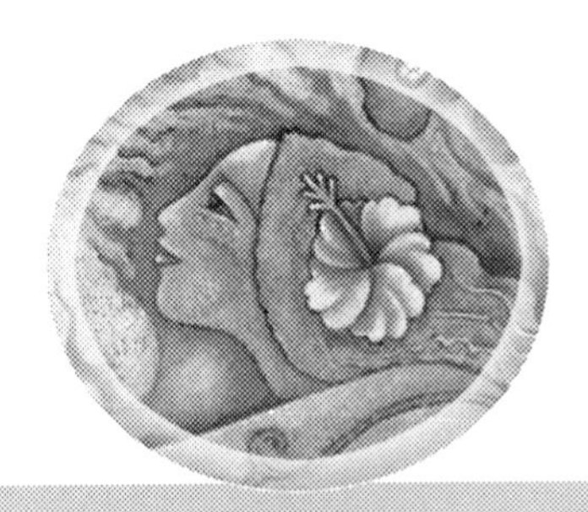

TURNING *your own* STONES

Get together with some girlfriends—in person or on-line—and ask yourselves these questions. You might want to write down the answers first, then share them with each other.

1. What kind of exercise, if any, are you currently doing, and is it something you love to do or something you think you "should" be doing?
2. When do you feel the most "beautiful"?
3. What are *you* hungry for?
4. What form of advertising and media can you eliminate from your life that would free you from a false sense of yourself?

5. What does the idea of "body as a temple" mean to you? How do you keep yours in good repair so that you can "dance, dance, dance"?

6. How do you get grounded?

3

Owning Your Emotions

◆

If only we'd stop trying to be happy, we could have a pretty good time.

—Edith Wharton, American novelist

UNVEILING EMOTIONS & FEELINGS

Not to completely feel is thinking.

—E. E. CUMMINGS, POET

- People talk about how love and cheerfulness and optimism are positive emotions, and sadness, fear, and anger are negative emotions, and negative emotions are dangerous. But my experience is that all emotions, to the extent that they engage you with life, are positive.

  —Rachel Naomi Remen in HEALING AND THE MIND, *Bill Moyers*

- Emotions are just energy in motion. When a violent storm erupts, it moves through the sky, then the sun comes out, and the world is a far more beautiful place than it was a few minutes ago.

  —Shane Orne, riding coach & mother

- Every emotion is a message about what's going on in our internal and external environment. Fear says, "It's not safe!" Anger says, "I'm being violated!"

Sadness says, "Something is lost." When we listen to our emotions, we receive important information to help us navigate through life.

—Sheryll Hirschberger, teacher, author & Feng Shui consultant

- No one else is responsible for the way you feel. It may seem as if someone else is making you feel bad, but the truth is that only you can be in charge of the way you respond.

—J&B

◆

E*motions are natural and healthy, not to be repressed or denied or ashamed of. They are all colors of the spectrum of a healthy emotional life.*

—JUNE KONPKA, ADDICTION COUNSELOR

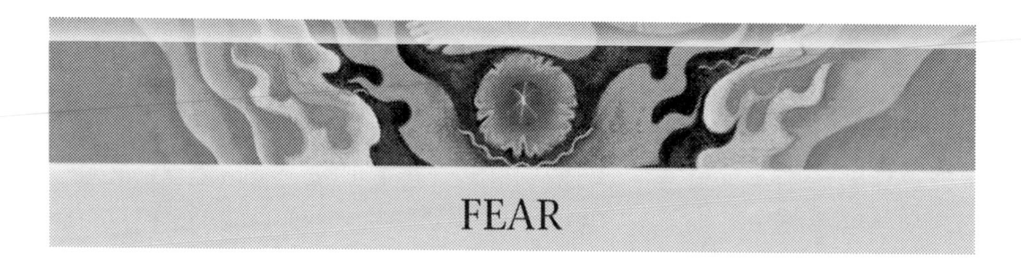

FEAR

Fear: The best way out is through.

—HELEN KELLER, SOCIAL ADVOCATE & REFORMER

- When fear comes up, I walk right into it, heading straight into the center. I don't turn my back on it or run away. I take a deep breath and go for it, saying the things I feel I need to say. I take responsibility if I've made a mistake, and am willing to do things without being afraid of the consequences, because honesty brings people close.

—Wanda Roth, fashion & jewelry consultant

- I have been so gripped by fear that I've been on my hands and knees crawling, but I kept going. What I'm afraid of shows me where I need to go. The only difference between a hero and a regular person is that the regular person fears and stops, and the hero doesn't stop.

—Sage Hamilton, community leader & women's group facilitator

- I say invite the monster in for tea. Look fear in the eye, ask it what it needs and requires from you, and how you can support what is needed.

—Wendy Bramlett, yoga teacher & studio owner

◆

F*ear makes strangers of people who should be friends.*

—SHIRLEY MACLAINE, ACTRESS

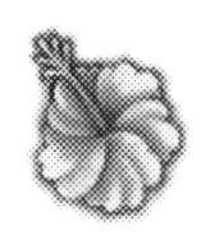

One morning while working on this book, I woke up with a knot in the pit of my stomach. I felt worried about the book—whether we were really doing it right, and whether we would be able to finish it on time. My impulse was to get up and do something—anything—to get rid of it.

Instead of getting up, I put my hands on my belly where the discomfort was strongest and let my attention rest on that spot. Then I let my breath flood that area. I got some relief, but not enough to convince me that it was working. So I was tempted again to get up and try something else, like doing yoga or showering it off—things I knew would ease the intensity.

But I hung in there, continuing to breathe and feel and listen. It was not easy; in fact, it took a lot of guts to stay with it when nothing in me was trusting the process. But slowly, staying with it, everything softened and I melted through to the other side. I discovered that on the other side of fear there is a deep, soft strength.

—BWH

LONELINESS

I *am never alone—I have myself!*

—SHAR LEE, YOGA TEACHER & CRANIAL THERAPIST

- Many believe that they need company at any cost, and certainly if a thing is desired at any cost, it will be obtained at all costs. We need to remember and to teach our children that solitude can be a much-to-be-desired condition. Not only is it acceptable to be alone, at times it is positively to be wished for. *—Maya Angelou, LOVING WHAT IS*

- What a lovely surprise to discover how un-lonely being alone can be. *—Ellen Burstyn, actress*

- I spent many years dwelling in loneliness. I was in a constant state of ache for someone or something that was missing. Eventually, I grew to understand the ache of loneliness as the cry of my own wounded heart. I learned I could soothe the pain with my own loving attention. I learned, much to my surprise, that nothing was missing. Loneliness led me to discover my own wholeness. And wholeness led me to a relationship with a man that is better than anything I could have imagined.

—Sheryll Hirschberger, teacher, author & Feng Shui consultant

- I reached out for love through my sexuality. I found that to be very lonely because neither I nor most of the people I reached out to knew anything about love. It was just a distraction from that feeling of loneliness.

—Terra Rafael, midwife & Ayurvedic practitioner

- We seem so frightened today of being alone that we never let it happen. . . . When the noise stops there is no inner music to take its place. We must relearn to be alone.

—Anne Morrow Lindberg, WOMEN'S SOLITUDE

◆

Solitude and solace are the same word. It means to soothe. To have solitude doesn't mean to be lonely.

—CLARISSA PINKOLA ESTES, *THEATER OF THE IMAGINATION*

GRIEF

Those who do not know how to weep
with their whole heart don't know how to laugh either.
—GOLDA MEIR, ISRAELI PRIME MINISTER

- The body is full of stuffed tears. Tears of grief and tears of rage and the stream makes the body cry. Then the body is ready to receive love.

  —Angeline Locey, Hawaiian healer, in
  NATIVE WISDOM FOR WHITE MINDS, Anne Wilson Schaef

- We don't take the time to grieve for the passing of cycles. My wish for all women is that we honor our losses by being present and even indulgent. Mourn for what has died in full.

  —Mukara Meredith, leadership consultant & community educator

- I am not an angry person, but I do grief and self-pity well. I had to learn the fine line between them. It is important to let yourself grieve for loss, to feel and allow those releases. But to indulge and wallow in self-pity is actually counterproductive for the clearing that transpires when you grieve and move on.

—Prema Rose, former Broadway actress, filmmaker & midwife

- When my best friend died suddenly, I was thrust into the unfamiliar territory of grief. I decided to honor my friend's life by fully grieving her death, even though I was terrified that the feelings would consume me. No matter what I experienced, I stayed with my heart's process. And I discovered a heart ripped open has a lot more surface area with which to feel love and compassion.

—Sheryll Hirschberger, teacher, author & Feng Shui consultant

◆

A *good cry lightens the heart.*

—YIDDISH PROVERB

JEALOUSY & ENVY

Jealousy is all the fun you think they had.

—ERICA JONG, AMERICAN WRITER & FEMINIST

- If you are jealous of someone, the important issue for you is not that specific person but the shadow side of your nature as it is reflected in that person. In effect, that person serves as your teacher. Concentrating on the person of whom you are jealous will not heal you. You will only be sent more and more teachers, each more intense than the previous one.

  —*Carolyn Myss, Anatomy of the Spirit*

- You know that jealousy is unreasonable. And you know that you can't possibly have all of another person's time and affection. . . . You know your lover needs other friends, other interests and time to be alone. You know that jealousy makes you ugly and weak. But the monster accepts no reasons—except the ones that feed your suspicions.

  —*Deborah Phillips, Sexual Confidence*

- Envy is one of the most instructive ways of seeing and becoming what you want to live more of in your life. It takes much trust and love to feel into another woman's beauty deeply enough to learn from it rather than suffer from it.

  —Jennifer Garcia, seminar leader & women's group facilitator

- Envy of another can be a huge compliment when confessed and the fastest working cancer when withheld. It can eat away at you as a woman and eat away at the relationship you experience it in. Sometimes sharing that envy with the other makes it possible to be liberated into greater trust and appreciation for each other.

  —Amy McCarrel, seminar leader & women's group facilitator

◆

Jealousy, that dragon which slays love
under the pretense of keeping it alive.

—HAVELOCK ELLIS, AUTHOR & PSYCHOLOGIST

ANGER

If you're angry, be angry and deal with it.
Don't go out and eat a bag of Ruffles.

—OPRAH WINFREY, TELEVISION TALK SHOW HOST

- Women have long been discouraged from the forthright expression of anger. Any woman who openly expresses anger at men is branded as unfeminine, unattractive or even strident and a shrew! But deep down there is a noble energy being kindled into a roaring fire. This explains why women have great powers of endurance and of love: for anger is close to love.

  —*Julian Sleigh, FRIENDS AND LOVERS*

- I considered my anger a flaw. I've come to realize it is part and parcel of a wide emotional range. I don't just have anger; I have a large and deep reservoir of feelings that I work with. I can't just pluck out anger and keep all the other emotions. I wouldn't want to be less passionate or emotional.

  —*Ellen Burstyn, ON WOMEN TURNING 50*

- To be a fully human and empowered woman, it is okay to feel anger. I really appreciate the things that make me angry, for they are always my guidance system. Anger is a great emotion when it is used elegantly.

—Christiane Northrup, M.D.

- Anger repressed can poison a relationship as surely as the cruelest words.

—Dr. Joyce Brothers, psychologist & television personality

♦

Don't hold on to anger, hurt or pain.
They steal your energy and keep you from love.

—LEO BUSCAGLIA, AUTHOR & MOTIVATIONAL SPEAKER

SHAME

Most Native people believe that our bodies were created by a most holy God, and how could anything made by the Creator be bad?

—ANNE WILSON SCHAEF, *NATIVE WISDOM FOR WHITE MINDS*

- By purposely remaining blind to these shameful, darker parts of ourselves, we become enslaved by the very parts we won't acknowledge. Those ugly blemishes you'd rather not have to see are just as much a part of you as the "good girl." That's not to say that the dark part of ourselves is in any way a permanent, indelible part of our makeup. Everything is subject to change.

  —Lynn Ginsburg & Mary Taylor, WHAT ARE YOU HUNGRY FOR?

- With all of the Western religious pressure to avoid sex, and because sex is seen as something that takes you away from God rather than to her, women are confused about their sexuality and have internalized this shame and conflict. We have been taught to disown a most integral aspect of our being, and when it arises in us as a natural desire or urge, we are told it's "bad."

—*Wind Hughes, Daughters of the Moon, Sisters of the Sun*

- The key to healing shame is to look at its source, what triggered it. Find the courage to speak about it. When we can name the thing we feel shame about, it alleviates much of the constriction. When we unburden our hearts, we open channels for support and camaraderie, connecting to a larger network of women who have all traveled the same path in their own way. By doing this, we come to learn that we are not alone in our experience of shame, and that we can heal from it.

—*Andrea Girman, women's health practitioner & pediatrician*

◆

Isn't it ironic that what we're discovering to be our greatest gifts— our spontaneity, our free expression, our sensuality and our feminine powers— are what we've had to suppress and be ashamed of for centuries.

—JANE KONOPKA, ADDICTION COUNSELOR

DEPRESSION

When it comes to depression, women have the right to sing the blues. The illness is twice as common in women as in men.

—MAYO CLINIC ON DEPRESSION

- If a woman is caught in an overextended lifestyle and achievement-oriented values, depression or illness may offer the only opportunity to allow her to be with herself. As she ignores her own need for quiet and self-nurture, the voice of the deeper Self may call through depression.

  —Judith Duerk, Circle of Stones

- It is estimated that only one out of three seriously depressed people ever seek treatment. The pain caused by this situation is needless. . . . Depression and bipolar disorders are treatable, and in many cases, can be cured.

  —Roberta Roesch, The Encyclopedia of Depression

- Depression serves a woman as it presses down on her, forcing her to leave behind that which was not of herself, which had influenced her to live a life alien to her own nature.

—*Judith Duerk,* CIRCLE OF STONES

◆

If you can't make your heart dance because you are too depressed, do something that makes someone else's heart dance. If you keep doing that for a couple of months, it changes your life. . . . One day perhaps we will get together and all dance.

—YOKO ONO, ARTIST & MUSICIAN

LOVE

Feelings are the holiest force in the universe (they are the only reason for life) and the feeling of love is the holiest of the holy.

—TERRY COLE-WHITTAKER, MOTIVATIONAL SPEAKER & AUTHOR

- The story of love is not important—what is important is that one is capable of love. It is perhaps the only glimpse we are permitted of eternity.

  —Helen Hayes, actress

- It doesn't matter where love comes from. If you're setting up conditions about where you want the love to flow from, you're just going to block it. When you realize that love is infinite, you can just let it flow through you, no matter what the source.

  —Catherine Carter, health educator

- No matter how much pain and sorrow we experience in life, I believe if we long for true love with all our heart, that longing must eventually lead us to our goal. One day, we will be able to look back and see and know that all of those seemingly difficult experiences were love. This will enable us to participate more consciously in this process called "life," that seems to me more like a continuously interweaving cycle of life, death and rebirth.

—Farida Sharan, Flower Child

- The Eskimo has fifty-two names for snow because it is important to them; there ought to be as many for love.

—Margaret Atwood, Canadian writer

◆

It is the loving, not the loved, woman who feels lovable.

—JESSAMYN WEST, ACTIVIST LIBRARIAN

DEALING *with* DEATH & LOSS

What is death? I don't know. I know beyond a shadow of a doubt that we survive this body.

—STEPHEN LEVINE IN *TYING ROCKS TO CLOUDS,* WILLIAM ELLIOTT

- Since before time you have been free. Birth and death are only doors through which we pass, sacred thresholds on our journey. Birth and death are a game of hide and seek. You have never been born and you never die. Our greatest pain is our notion of coming and going.

  —Thich Nhat Hanh, No Death, No Fear

- Death is a graduation. When we've taught all the things we came to teach, learned all the things we came to learn, then we're allowed to graduate. Some children die and graduate very early. Their sole reason to come was to be a teacher for moms and dads, usually, or for a brother or sister. Then they're allowed to go back home.

  —Dr. Elisabeth Kubler-Ross in Tying Rocks to Clouds, William Elliott

- We can't really know personally what we will meet on the other side—that's faith and belief. Everyone develops her/his own picture of what it might be. It is in the language and experience of gospel music that I take heart. I imagine the passing of life into death as a going to glory. *Glory,* what a concept! I can feel it with my imagination—pure, unadulterated radiance.

  —Valerie Stricklett, sculptor & human services administrator

- Death is my greatest inspiration in life. Death teaches nonattachment, because in death we can't take anything with us. Every moment we have to be ready to let go of everything we think we have or think we are, and that includes our relationships, our minds, even our bodies—and look for that which never dies. When we find that, we know that even a relationship ending is also just another opportunity to learn the art of letting go.

  —Deva Premal, singer & musician

◆

T*his alone is to be feared—the closed mind, the sleeping imagination, the death of the spirit. The death of the body is to that, I think, a little thing.*

—WINIFRED HOLTBY, NOVELIST & FEMINIST WRITER

TRUSTING *your* FEELINGS

A woman who cannot honor her own feelings will not find them honored by anyone else.

—MARIANNE WILLIAMSON, *A WOMAN'S WORTH*

- As women, we often have strong bodily feelings and a deep inner knowingness. Then we are talked out of it by ourselves or others. Sometimes it can be a male who does not want us to know the truth. We think we are crazy. We feel bad for feeling what we're feeling, for example, that they're cheating on us or lying to us. But when the truth is finally revealed, we realize that we had sensed it all along. This a gift we have. Learn to use and trust it. It can save your life in many ways.

  —*Indigo Margolis, minister, counselor & poet*

- Don't be in denial. Acknowledge the truth of what you feel. That's an unbelievably important step. But it's a worthless step if you don't take the second step, saying to yourself: Given that I am in despair, how do I now move on with love?

—DH, business & family manager

- Real feelings are experienced in the moment. But the second we connect a feeling to a thought, we can no longer access our true feelings, because thought takes us out of the present moment, into the past or future. Stop listening to the content of the thought, and start to recognize where it takes you in time and space. Then choose to come back to the present. This is self-powerment.

  —Faye Mandell, mother & coach

◆

If you are never scared, embarrassed or hurt, it means you never take chances.

—JULIA SOUL, ACTRESS

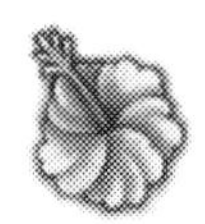

The DIAMOND MINE:
What would you do if you only had one day to live?

- If I had only one day to live I would just completely surrender myself as much as was physically possible to live every second of that day with the most open heart I have. I'd be with people I love. And I'd be there as fully and completely and as rawly as I possibly, possibly could.

  —Sue Huggins, full-time mother

- I'd want friends and family with me. I would love to feed the senses together . . . eating, listening to music, touching, caressing each other. The theme of the day would be gratitude. I would love to talk about everything I'm grateful for and give those around me the chance to express whatever they needed to express to have my passing be a blessing for them. There's a chair and a window in my house. If I could orchestrate this, I'd love to be in that chair with the winter morning sun on my face.

—Holly Moore, artist & mother

- Meditate, dance, play, love and then meditate again.

  —Shari Hindman, healer, mother & businesswoman

- I would be on a tropical beach with my husband, eating mangoes, swimming with dolphins, watching the clouds go by while lying in a hammock. I would spend the day connected to nature at its finest. In the evening I would have a banquet with my closest friends and family. Then I'd have the Agape International Gospel Choir perform, then have a live Latin salsa dance band and dance until I dropped. Then I'd be cremated and have my ashes sent up over the ocean in a massive fireworks display.

  —Arielle Ford, media relations expert & author

- I could die right now. I've done everything I want to do. If I had one day, I'd be at the beach, which always reminds me of who I truly am. I would feel gratitude for everybody and everything, being with the wind, the water, the sand, the sky and the sun's kisses. There isn't anything I feel I've missed out on. I'm only thirty-six, but there's nothing I feel compelled to do or need to do before I die.

  —Jennifer Claire Moyer, actress

- I would make love, eat rich foods, take a bath and make love again. I'd celebrate all the things I enjoy doing in my body, because that's what I'd be leaving behind.

—Sheryll Hirschberger, therapist, writer & Feng Shui consultant

- I would wake up early in the morning and walk in the woods with my husband David. I would talk about our life together over the last thirty years. In the mid-morning I would find my daughter, and watch her dance a piece she had choreographed. Then I would have lunch at the Court of Two Sisters in New Orleans with the five most important women in my life and my sister, and it would last all day. We would tell our favorite stories of our triumphs, our embarrassments, our children and ourselves. And we would eat everything on the menu! In the late afternoon I would paint one last painting. It would be fast and loose—the way I've always wanted to paint—and it would be full of color and contain everything I know about painting. Then I would walk up to the highest vista on my North Carolina land and watch the sunset.

—Pamela George, Ph.D., professor & painter

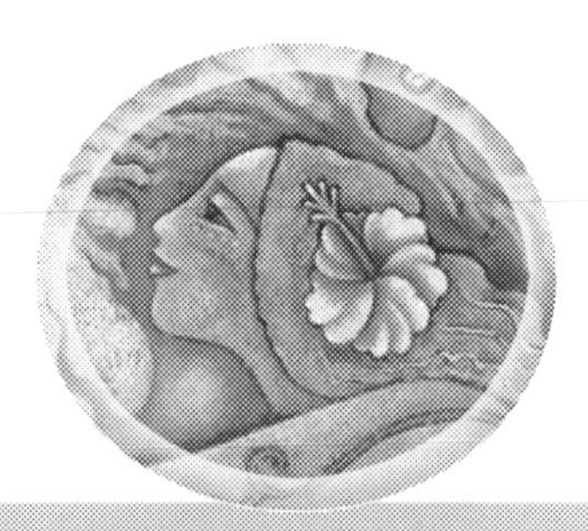

STEPPING-STONES *for* OWNING *your* EMOTIONS

- I have found that the most efficient route back to personal integrity is feeling my feelings. I need to face my emotional castaways, such as shame, anger and fear. Whether you explore this with a spiritually-oriented therapist, or a friend, or in the quiet of your meditations, bring to awareness whatever stands between you and the effortless alignment with what you feel in your heart in each moment.

  —Wendy Grace Danner, metaphysical teacher & counselor

- If your emotions are stuck, move with them. Tears are movement, dance is movement, nature is movement. Water is a great conduit for bringing the emotions into balance. Float in any body of water—the ocean, the tub. Make a shift from thinking to feeling and you have made a giant step in freeing up and creating your own destiny.

—Peggy Watson, dolphin facilitator & swim coach

- After I had surgery for breast cancer, it turned out that I had to go to work. It was one of the best things that could have happened to me, because I had something to put my attention on rather than self-pity.

  —Maureen Read, seniors tennis player

- Move your attention into your heart, then with each breath, imagine your heart expanding, so that it gets as big as your body, the room, the house, the community, the state, the country and the world. With each breath, as your heart expands, you'll find very quickly that there's nothing outside your heart. You move to a universal level, where there is no fear, no loneliness, no feeling of angst or separation. You can do this with your eyes closed or while being active, because you're always breathing!

  —Amsheva Mallani, healer & teacher

- Write! Anyone can write; no one should be afraid of that process. I started writing when I was ten or twelve years old. As soon as that magic happened, there was no way to back away from it. I found out over the years that writing is a tool that actually stabilizes my emotional well-being.

  —Hilary Kurtz, publisher & editor

- Sometimes being out of balance emotionally is simply the result of not being rested enough. Getting enough rest/sleep is one of the easiest and most economical ways to regain balance.

  —J&B

- FEAR. Before you go to do anything you are afraid of, take ten really deep long, slow breaths. This will get you out of your head where fear has its residence and into your body, into the present where fear cannot live.

  —Nita Desai, M.D., & Ayurvedic practitioner

- FEAR. I offer fear to God, just ask him to take it from me. It sounds trite, but it has really made a difference for me. For example, my husband was expressing discomfort about work, and I felt terror about the possibility of losing an important employee. I recognized the fear, then reminded myself that I had no control over the situation, and also, that if it happened, things were still going to be all right. I realize that there's a bigger reason for everything happening that I don't see most of the time.

  —Nancy Leahy, mother & nature lover

- FEAR. I go to the place where I feel fear in my body. It usually feels like space that has been greatly compressed, like I'm holding on very tightly. The color is usually black, but in the center, very faint, there is a spark of light. I expand the light until there is no darkness left. Then the fear is revealed as light.

  —Rebecca Hudson, rock-climbing instructor & mother

- Loneliness. If I feel lonely, I know that I need to open my heart and actively love other people. Opening my heart means I go inside my body with my attention and release the clamp that's around my physical heart. Then I open my eyes and notice how every human being is needing acknowledgement and love. So I am just naturally drawn to giving some time, attention and energy to someone else. It's a magical cure.

  —Sheila Ross, mother, wife & community leader

- Death. I was surprised to discover how many people would rather not talk about death. For me, sharing stories of death is one of the best ways to navigate through it.

  —SARK, The Bodacious Book of Succulence

- Anger. If people were taught right when they were young, they would be taught what natural emotions are. Cry when you're sad! Stamp your foot! Beat something up, but not a living thing! Take a piece of rubber hose and shred a telephone book to pieces. Then, you won't have to beat your kids; you won't have to kick your dog, bash up your wife or husband. Anger is a natural emotion. It gets destructive only when it's like a pressure cooker that erupts.

  —Dr. Elisabeth Kubler-Ross, Tying Rocks to Clouds, William Elliott

- Anger. Know that anger in someone else is an appeal for help and healing. Don't match energies. Just keep breathing, and after they have finished, ask, "How can I support you?"

  —Sondra Ray, Loving Relationships

- SHAME. . . . Here is what to do about shame-filled secrets. . . . See what you see. Say it to someone. It is never too late. If you feel you cannot say it aloud, write it down for them. Choose a person whom you instinctively believe to be trustworthy. The can of worms you are worried about opening is far better off being out there than festering inside yourself. If you prefer, seek a therapist who knows how to deal with secrets.

  —Clarissa Pinkola Estes, WOMEN WHO RUN WITH THE WOLVES

- DEPRESSION. The women I have seen who are the most depressed usually don't have enough progesterone. Using birth control pills is also associated with depression. If you practice birth control, research natural birth control methods and have your hormone levels tested.

  —Maurieke Shyelle, M.D. & women's health practitioner

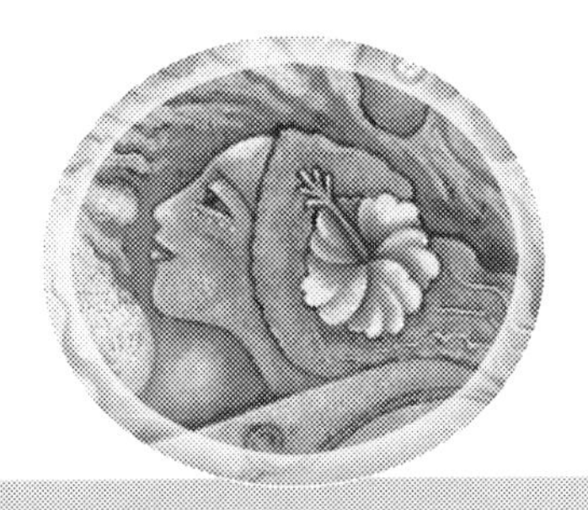

TURNING *your own* STONES

Get together with some girlfriends—in person or on-line—and ask yourselves these questions. You might want to write down the answers first, then share them with each other.

1. Which troublesome emotion would you be willing to "invite for tea" and dialogue with?

2. What are you envying that you would like to become more of in your life and what would be a first step in fulfilling that?

3. What has been left unspoken or uncommunicated that you feel ashamed of, and who would be the most trusted person to share that with?

4. What are you holding onto in your life that is "dying"? Are you willing to let go and make room for something else to be born?

5. What would you do if you had only one day to live?

4

Getting Real About Relationships

◆

We are in relationship with everything,
from a blade of grass to the farthest star
and everything in between.
We cannot not *be in relationship.*

—Tamara Matthews, therapist

THE MOST IMPORTANT RELATIONSHIP

The most enlightened prayer isn't "Dear God, send me someone wonderful," but, "Dear God, help me realize that I am someone wonderful."

—MARIANNE WILLIAMSON, *A WOMAN'S WORTH*

- I walked for miles at night along the beach, composing bad blank verse and searching endlessly for someone wonderful who would step out of the darkness and change my life. It never crossed my mind that that person could be me.

  —Anna Quindlen, writer

- My self is my best friend. In my twenties, I had a terrifying realization that I was going to spend the rest of my existence with myself, and not even death was going to save me from that. I was never going to get away from me. I was terrified! But that put everything into perspective for me. I realized that I was the constant in the equation of my life.

  —Glynda Yoder, business owner

- Your relationship with yourself comes first. All others are secondary. If you look for love from somebody else and you don't love yourself, you will never feel safe and secure in that relationship. When in relationship, you have to continue to nurture the relationship you have with yourself.

  —Yaniyah Pearson, youth leadership director

- I spent the first half of my life trying to make my life fit into a relationship, rather than allowing relationship to support what I wanted for my own life in the large scheme of things. *—Ellen Greene, classics professor*

- Enjoy being alone. Then enjoy being together. This is the perfect relationship. Love yourself first, raise yourself higher and be shining. Then you will attract the partner who is suitable to your highest state.

  —Gayuna Cealo, Burmese monk & humanitarian

Then, it seemed time to be in union with myself, so I performed a metaphorical marriage, and promised to love and honor myself until the end.

—SARK, *SUCCULENT WILD WOMAN*

RELATIONSHIPS *as* MIRRORS

A *partner will bring up all your patterns. Don't avoid relationships: they are the best seminar in town. The truth is that your partner is your guru.*

—SONDRA RAY, *LOVING RELATIONSHIPS*

- A problem in a relationship is never about the other person. The people in your life are not there out of happenstance—they're there as a reflection of what you need to learn about yourself. For example, I had a problem with the stepmother of one of my sons. But I knew it was only about me needing to forgive her. It had nothing to do with her.

  —*Shane Orne, riding coach & mother*

- When you fall in love, and six months later find that the things you loved about the person are now the things you no longer love—or that even aggravate you—that's when the fun begins. That's when you have to look at yourself and ask, "What is there for me in this situation to learn about myself?"

  —*Wanda Roth, fashion & jewelry consultant*

- Relationships serve the individual—not the other way around. Through the process of coming together, you get to be a mirror for another person. My "work" is simply allowing people to be who they are, rather than thinking that I have the template and would you please adjust!

  —Dawn Hunter, organic gardener, dancer & fiber artisan

- Nothing can stop our parents from pushing our buttons! How you react to them is a great gauge of how much work you've done—and how much you still have to do.

  —Tamara Matthews, therapist

◆

When we receive a lot of love from someone, the stuff unlike love will come out of us in the form of anger, sadness, fear, pain, upset and all other suppressed negativity. Our partners are healing us by pushing this negativity out of us.

—SONDRA RAY, *LOVING RELATIONSHIPS*

BEING HONEST

The best mind-altering drug is truth.

—LILY TOMLIN, ACTRESS & COMEDIENNE

- To me real honesty means expressing who you are all the time each step of the way. Be clear. Using this approach avoids the buildup of problems that have festered. When repressed emotions explode due to lack of honesty, they can become "the last straw," and they can take everyone, including you, by surprise. Creating a habit of being honest will also give you a great deal of self-knowing and self-empowerment.

—Barbara Foster, artist & Vedic astrologer

- There's a wonderful Old English definition of the word "courage": "To speak your mind by telling all your heart."

—Carol Gilligan, DAUGHTERS OF THE MOON, SISTERS OF THE SUN

- Our greatest fear is that the truth will be abhorrent to our lover and we will end up alone. The reality is that the longer we are together and the more we practice the truth, the more trust develops and the easier truth becomes. When we hide nothing, we can give everything.

  —Julia & Kenny Loggins,
  The Unimaginable Life: Lessons learned on the Path of Love

- You have to be truly honest about what you feel so that you can express that to your partner. Communication is the ultimate between any two people.

  —Marsha Wright, marketing account executive

◆

T*he truth is the kindest thing we can give people in the end.*

—HARRIET BEECHER STOWE, SOCIAL REFORMER & AUTHOR

FEMALE FRIENDSHIPS

There was a definite process by which one made people into friends, and it involved talking to them and listening to them for hours at a time.

—REBECCA WEST, ENGLISH WRITER

- It's as though each of the friends I have in my life is a different color, and when we put them all together, with different shapes and shades, we end up with a patchwork quilt that is a place in which to curl up in comfort.

  —Sharon Wegscheider-Cruse, Girl Talk

- Almost every friendship I had . . . developed problems. One or both of us was afraid to go into the darkness together, to speak our truths and to describe our experience. These truths would have been oxygen—some of my friendships ended by suffocation. I would be so afraid of losing a friend that I didn't tell the truth and would lose her anyway.

  —SARK, Succulent Wild Woman

- I have learned so much from, and been held in such deeply profound ways by women, especially in my darkest hours. I feel a critical part of being a woman is having deeply connected female relationships. The richness of these interactions only enhances my relationship with my male partner. There are ways of nurturing and being nurtured that I just cannot derive from relationships with men. Having friendships with women of all ages is so important. It's our nature as women and our lifeline.

—Andrea Girman, women's health practitioner & pediatrician

◆

Each friend represents a world in us, a world possibly not born until they arrive, and it is only by this meeting that a new world is born.

—ANAÏS NIN, AMERICAN (FRENCH-BORN) AUTHOR

I have a twin sister. We were very close but came to a point where we couldn't even talk to each other. When we did reconnect it was very superficial and non-intimate. I took a workshop that recommended developing women friends and enjoying their company. This meant *really* listening to them, who they are and what they are up to. I started doing that with my sister and within a week this listening *totally* transformed our relationship. She was more interested in me and I in her. Relationships I think are first about listening.

—Name withheld

FEMALE/MALE POLARITY

The unifying of opposites is the eternal process.

—MARY PARKER FOLLETT, MANAGEMENT PIONEER

- In intimate relationships with men, I want to major in feminine and minor in masculine. At a lecture podium, I'm the masculine, active energy to the audience's feminine receptiveness. After work, if I'm with a man I am close to, I want to experience myself as a woman. And I no longer kid myself that it would work for him, or for me, to play it any differently. That doesn't mean we don't trade roles at times. It means the dominant groove is that he's masculine and I'm feminine.

  —*Marianne Williamson, A Woman's Worth*

- A challenge for many women around relationship is that they think, "If I don't make this happen, it won't happen." This is the opposite of the truth. When a woman is in her divine nature, inwardly sensual, radiant and full of feminine intelligence, she will attract—she will never have to go out in search of a partner.

—Wanda Roth, fashion & jewelry consultant

- Your ability to activate your polarity is available at any moment. Do whatever it takes to transform yourself in the moment by reaching for fullness and beauty—take a bath, run in the grass, adorn yourself, dance.

  —Jennifer Garcia, seminar leader & women's group facilitator

- I experience myself as an androgynous being that has the availability of both principles of creation, male and female, within. It's been my journey to harness that energy, balance it and understand it. I've experienced myself as male energy, with male attitudes and values, and seek to understand and explore that. And I've experienced my infinite nature as a woman and as a feminine energy. I have learned to go back to the soul level of recognition and understanding and accept the essence of my being.

  —Lilli Botchis, Ph.D., alchemical researcher & adviser

Both masculine and feminine play within us all. In an ever-changing dance, male and female intertwine, finding fulfillment in the heart.

—J&B

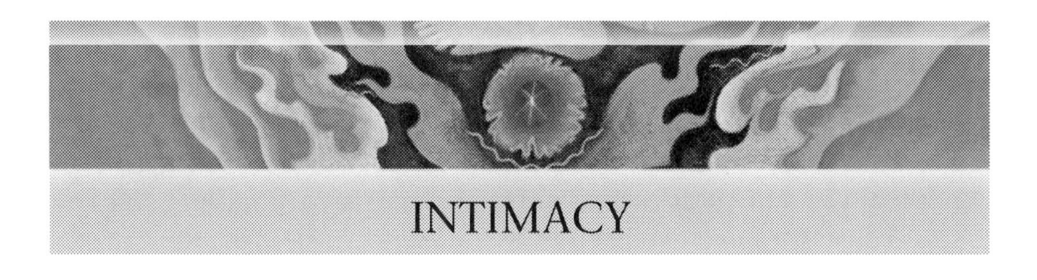

INTIMACY

Even as one part of us seeks to be an individual, another part longs to restore the safety and comfort of merging with another.

—GAIL SHEEHY, WRITER

- Don't confuse "having sex" with "making love." There's nothing wrong with either one. But no amount of candles, wine and Quincy Jones will turn sex into real romance. Sex for the sake of sex can be frolicking fun. But making love only occurs when you are open and present, from the deepest reaches of who you really are.

  —Judith Sherven, Ph.D., & James Sniechowski, Ph.D., The New Intimacy

- Go slow sexually. Going fast probably causes more suffering than anything else, especially for women. The attraction is so strong that people go for it, and it's such a high that it's a contrast to the suffering most of us carry throughout our lives. Sex often looks like intimacy, and we rush to it because we're so hungry for depth and connectedness. Before you know it, somebody's pregnant!

—Name withheld

- In relationship, whatever happens is always your own responsibility. It's not that you don't judge others or blame them, because it's human to do that. But it's the next step that makes a difference. Instead of pulling away, criticizing or withdrawing to avoid intimacy, ask yourself , "What is this person mirroring for me?" Then you can reflect on yourself and see if you can take a step in a new direction. It might be anger, or actually speaking up for yourself or even saying something that feels mean. But give an honest response, and you will go to the next step in your intimacy.

—DH, business & family manager

The easiest kind of relationship with me
is with ten thousand people. The hardest is with one.

—JOAN BAEZ, SINGER

COMMITMENT

A successful marriage takes falling in love many times, always with the same person.

—MIGNON MCLAUGHLIN, U.S. JOURNALIST & AUTHOR

- You've got to be willing to stay committed to someone over the long run, and sometimes it doesn't work out. But often if you become real honest with yourself and honest with each other, and put aside whatever personal hurt and disappointment you have to really understand yourself and your spouse, it can be the most wonderful experience you've ever had.

  —Hillary Rodham Clinton, American First Lady

- I don't have a problem with people living together, but my experience is that these days it is too easy to just walk away when things get rough. It is a statement of how things are in this country—people just want to pop a pill to feel good rather than really committing to going to the depths of their situations for real healing and growing. Relationships are not always fun, not always easy. When you make a commitment in a marriage, it's important to really consider what you are doing, what you are signing up for.

—Donna Baase, cosmetic business owner, esthetician & educator

- It is natural to be in relationship. As long as you're alive, you must be in relationship. But to be in relationship is to experience both ecstasy and betrayal—and everything in between. If you can't accept this full range of emotion in relationship, it's better to withdraw from the world and be a nun.

—Eileen Dannemann, social activist

◆

You trace the lines in your beloved's face and you know that you put some of them there. This is commitment.

—PEGGY WATSON, DOLPHIN FACILITATOR & SWIM COACH

CHANGING OTHERS

To think that I know what's best for anyone else is to be out of my business. Even in the name of love, it is pure arrogance, and the result is tension, anxiety and fear. Do I know what's right for myself? That is my only business.

—BYRON KATIE, *LOVING WHAT IS*

- Trying to change someone is trying to make them more like you, as if there's something wrong with them. Instead of trying to change them, ask yourself why a certain behavior bothers you, when it may not bother anybody else. You could be unconsciously recognizing a behavior in yourself that you've left buried for many years.

  —Christine Bokelman, sign language interpreter

- Getting involved with the "wrong men"—those unable to engage in a stable relationship—caused me to waste a lot of time. I expended a lot of energy trying to "fix" these relationships, work on them all the time, trying to change these men so that they would be people who could be emotionally stable and reliable. I didn't focus enough on myself and my own development.

—Ellen Greene, classics professor

- When you want to set boundaries for someone else, it simply reflects your own limitations. It's so much easier to say there's something wrong with another person. But there's really no fault, no wrong—there's only growth.

  —Wanda Roth, fashion & jewelry consultant

- When I am trusting and being myself as fully as possible, everything in my life relfects this by falling into place easily, often miraculously.

  —Shakti Gawain, author

◈

N*o matter how much I give or how hard I try, I can't fix anyone else. However, I can create a safe, loving space for them to grow whole in. Where there is love, miraculous things happen.*

—SHERYLL HIRSCHBERGER, TEACHER, AUTHOR & FENG SHUI CONSULTANT

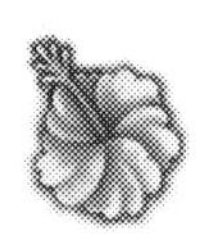

My husband and I had always planned that he would take a second career and I would stop working as a dental hygienist after we had raised five children and he retired from the service. But after twenty-two years in the service, he was forced to retire with a disability, and all our plans for "the future" disappeared. For ten years I tried to nurse his wounds and ease his suffering, until one day I found myself saying, "This is the direction I'm going to go in now—up. It's where I need to go, and I'd like you to come with me, but if you can't, I have to go anyway." My letting go was the turning point for my wounded knight to get back up on his horse again.

—Mary Cave, life coach

IS LOVE ENOUGH?

Love is not enough. It must be the foundation,
the cornerstone—but not the complete structure.

—BETTE DAVIS, ACTRESS

- We need more than love to make love last.

—Nathaniel Branden & E. Devers Branden, authors

- Love is not enough. Listening skills are the key to healthy, successful relationships. Listening and acknowledging, sharing and communicating are tools that allow love to be cultured. I can love a lot of people in an abstract way, but when I'm right in there with someone and it gets tough, the skill to staying in intimacy is the ability to listen.

—Terra Rafael, midwife & Ayurvedic practitioner

- Unequivocally no! I spent years studying about this, then years writing and teaching about it. My experience says there needs to be enough compatibility of values, habits and ways of interacting with people that will make for a positive, long-term relationship. We all fall in and out of love all the time. Unless there is compatibility between the partners, the marriage will not survive.

  —Joan Lescinski, CSJ, Ph.D., president, Saint-Mary-of-the-Woods College

- My husband and I have been married for twenty years. What has seen us through the ups and downs of relationship is our commitment to ride the waves. There is a thrill in looking deep into each others' eyes and seeing the history between us, the years of growing together, parenting together. I am learning that the joy is not in achieving "the ideal relationship" but in receiving what comes in relationship.

  —Diana Krystofiak, environmental advocate

Love doesn't just sit there like a stone,
it has to be made, like bread; re-made all the time, made new.

—URSULA K. LE GUIN, AUTHOR

MARRIAGE & EXPECTATIONS

Love has nothing to do with what you are expecting to get—only what you are expecting to give—which is everything.

—KATHARINE HEPBURN, ACTRESS

- You don't have goals and expectations of your family, you just accept them for who they are. What if you could have that ease and acceptance with your marriage partner—he's family too! I am so much happier without "shoulds" and expectations of my husband and myself.

  —Alexis Mayne, president, natural cosmetics company

- The whole pattern of expectation is set in motion the moment you "want," "require" or "need" the other to fulfill something in you. This sets the stage for resentment and fault finding in the relationship. If you can drop your expectations both of yourself and the other, then you're both free to blossom.

  —Kiki Matthews, sales executive & nutritionist

- I thought I married for love, but I was twenty-nine, and still very, very young. We'd only known each other a year. What a rude awakening! Now I'm single and about to turn fifty, and I really don't care about getting married. What I care about is having a real relationship—having a devotion that just comes naturally with my partner, and deep ease, and friendship and commonality, which is not something I even considered when I was getting married.

  —Hilary Kurtz, publisher & editor

- True intimacy is frightening, and I was well into my marriage before I realized that I either had to seek it or live a lie. Intimacy is what makes a marriage, not a ceremony, not a piece of paper from the state.

  —Kathleen Norris, author

◆

I used to believe that marriage would diminish me, reduce my options. That you had to be someone less to live with someone else when, of course, you have to be someone more.

—CANDICE BERGEN, ACTRESS

HAVING KIDS

On a deeply personal level, the birth of my children was extraordinary. The miraculous renewal of life and hope and faith in the possibilities of the future will never leave me.

—QUEEN NOOR AL HUSSEIN,
A&E BIOGRAPHY, QUEEN NOOR: BETWEEN TWO REALMS

- It is not until you become a mother that your judgment slowly turns to compassion and understanding.

  —*Erma Bombeck, author*

- We don't have to give birth to children to know we're the mothers of the world. We are the wombs of the generations that follow, not only physically but emotionally, psychologically, and spiritually. . . . We are all mothers to all children.

  —*Marianne Williamson, A Woman's Worth*

- If you already are a young mother, don't let go of your dreams and goals no matter how difficult the situation may seem. I have found that there is always a way to create what we need. It may not be apparent how at the moment, and it may not happen in the time frame that we'd like, but a solution is out there. Be creative and believe in yourself.

  —Wind Hughes, Daughters of the Moon, Sisters of the Sun

- Regarding men and sexuality, I was always thinking about what felt good in the moment. I kept thinking I had all the time in the world to have children—that I didn't have to think in terms of the long-term. All of a sudden, I realized that I was up against the wall, that time had run out, and I had to come to terms with that.

  —Ellen Greene, classics professor

- I found out at age seventeen that I couldn't have children. I was heartbroken, but since then I've learned there are many ways to parent. I have helped raise two amazing stepchildren, love spending time with my nieces and nephews, have a passion for mentoring, and feel as though I'm giving birth every time a new book comes out!

  —JRH

- One thing you must think about when you're thinking about having children is what it is going to be like the day they get out of the feet pajamas, the day they are no longer adorable. It is tough. If you just want a wonderful little creature to love, you can get a puppy.

—*Barbara Walters in* The Successful Woman, *Dr. Joyce Brothers*

- Having a child later in life, you don't have the same energy as you did, but the advantages for me have far outweighed the disadvantages. I really wanted a child, and both my husband and I had lived a very active youth, fulfilling all our desires to be out in the world. I think the key is being very clear that that is what you are ready for. Parenting should be a very conscious choice and made for the right reasons.

  —*Jan Kleinborg, women's health practitioner & nurse*

- Have kids no matter what difficulties you see other parents going through—it's worth it!

  —*Wendy Read, reconciliation analyst & fabric artist*

There is a time when you have to explain to your children why they're born, and it's a marvelous thing if you know the reason by then.

—HAZEL SCOTT, AMERICAN-WEST INDIAN PIANIST

What I learned through becoming Fabien's mother was total acceptance and no expectation. I knew nothing about Down syndrome people, but at twenty-three I delivered a Down syndrome boy. I refused to read books about it; I just took one step at a time. We saw the people we needed to see, like physical therapists, in order for his development to be smooth and at the optimum pace, but I didn't want to put all kinds of preconceived ideas or limitations in my mind. So anything he accomplished was like having the heavens open up. The first time he sat up, I cried. That taught me wonder. It also helped me with my other children to come—just to let them be who they are.

—Marie-Helene Tourenne, fabric designer & mother

KNOWING *when to* LEAVE

Success lies in being able to retreat at the right moment and in the right manner. The success is made positive by the fact that the retreat is not the forced flight of a weak person but the voluntary withdrawal of a strong one.

—THE I CHING

- The last thing a woman wants to do is leave off the possibility of loving or being loved. So we stay. There's a lot of wisdom in staying and trying to reach higher ground. But if you're not going to higher ground, it may be time to look at alternatives.

  —Hilary Kurtz, publisher & editor

- I often ask groups of women, "How many of you have stayed in a situation much longer that you should have because you were afraid? You knew it was time to leave, you were called to do something else, but you just couldn't mobilize." Almost every hand goes up. We stay too long. We stay out of compassion. We stay out of fear. We stay out of a hundred different motivations. We don't follow our hearts. And, in a way, you can say that courage—from the French root *coeur,* which means "heart"—is following your heart.

—Joan Borysenko, Women of Spirit

- For years I thought about leaving my marriage because I felt "unloved." I've finally learned to love myself, to give to myself, to care for my body, to listen inwardly, to trust myself, to value myself and my gifts. To my surprise and enjoyment, what I've found is that self-love attracts love.

  —Diana Krystofiak, environmental advocate

- I was working at a shelter. *No one has the right to abuse you* was our mantra. That was news to many women. We have a right to say, "No, you may not abuse me, and if you have a need to denigrate me, then we're going to end this relationship."

  —Joan Lescinski, CSJ, Ph.D., president, Saint-Mary-of-the-Woods College

◆

Don't you want to know love? If so, then you must shepherd this relationship through its difficult periods. The growth that comes from staying with a friend far outweighs the benefits of the temporary break in the storm you get from leaving.

—HUGH & GAYLE PRATHER, *I WILL NEVER LEAVE YOU*

I've been married twenty-seven years. There were times in that marriage—sometimes two years at a time—when the friction was so intense I could not get my heart open. But was that the time to leave? No. Because I would never have gotten to the greatest place a woman could ever get to, which is to come out the other side, and find out what it feels like to be with the same man for thirty years.

And what was the good grace that let me hang in there? For me it was just God's grace, an answer to my ardent prayer, "Someone tell me what to do." We worked with a counselor, we did all kinds of things, and we got through it all.

If you think there might be something out there that could be helpful, at least give it a stab. What I have developed with my husband is a gift beyond all gifts, beyond anything I ever imagined it could have been.

—Sue Huggins, full-time mother

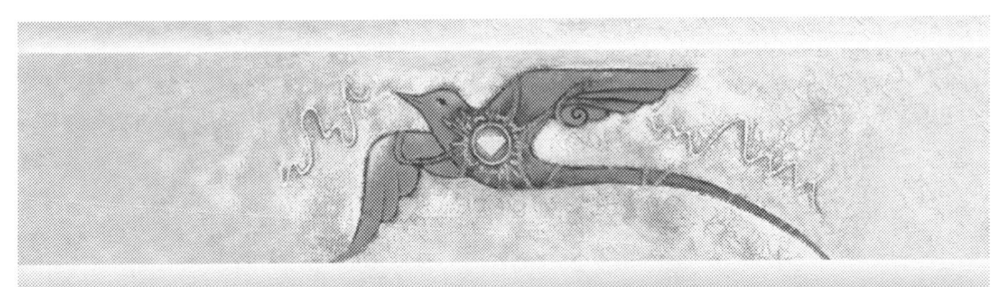

The DIAMOND MINE & STEPPING-STONES: *What's the most important thing you've learned about relationships?*

[EDITORS' NOTE: *We have combined* Stepping-Stones *and* The Diamond Mine *in this chapter. We found that the most important things women have learned about relationships are in fact stepping-stones to having happier and more empowered relationships.*]

- Enjoy the space between them.

  —Sue Berkey, yoga teacher & mother

- Never start an important discussion at bedtime.

  —JRH

- Most people are not listened to. If you want to do something for someone else, instead of talking, just listen to them.

  —Christine Bokelman, sign language interpreter

- I wish I had stayed more in self-authority. In my second marriage, I allowed my husband to take away my positivity and confidence. Before that, I had always been aware of my self-worth. But I became unable to make decisions and felt incompetent. You know the truth of who you are—so don't buy into anyone else trying to tell you or convince you that you are less than that.

—Carol Richter, spiritual counselor

- Two of the most liberating understandings I have had around intimate relationships with men are: (1) that men are not women, and women are not men; and (2) that my male partner is not supposed to be everything to me. These insights have helped me increasingly celebrate the differences between men and women, rather than dishonor or resent them. To complete what may feel missing in a relationship with an intimate partner, augment it with meaningful female friendships.

—Andrea Girman, women's health practitioner & pediatrician

- In my relationship, we have cultured the ability to circulate between roles as partners without ideas of how it *should be*. We allow a lot of space and don't assume we need to always sleep together or be any certain way together. We can be passionate or best friends or do our own thing. The cultural tendency is for the woman to be the one that is always poised and ready to design her life and energy around her spouse. You can be open and available without assuming that it's your exclusive role.

—Wendy Bramlett, yoga teacher & studio owner

- I would not have gone on so long thinking, "Surely this will get better."

—Stacey Hurlin, artist & community leader

- I hold all relationships as sacred. This means that I hold you as important, and that I will look out for your best interests. I will give you everything I have in terms of advice or support. Relationship is the complete absence of judgment of another as bad or incompetent.

—Rosie Estrin, healer & counselor

- Get relationship skills—and get them early in life. We're not born with them! Take advantage of the experts—don't just go to your friends.

—Tamara Matthews, therapist

- Don't let relationships be the center of your life. Keep your whole life in balance—friends, body, family, spirit, learning, playing.

—Diana Wald, artist & general contractor

- It's important to be able to discuss your relationship with God.

  —Heather Sanders, educator, wife & mother

- Sometimes I wonder if men and women really suit each other. Perhaps they should live next door and just visit now and then.

  —Katharine Hepburn, actress

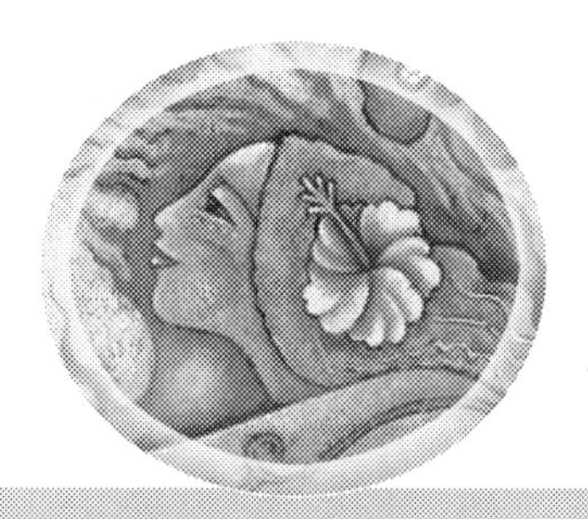

TURNING *your own* STONES

Get together with some girlfriends—in person or on-line—and ask yourselves these questions. You might want to write down the answers first, then share them with each other.

1. Write vows to yourself for your own metaphorical wedding. How will you love, honor and cherish yourself?

2. Whom are you not being honest with in relationship and how would honesty liberate you both?

3. What are some of the ways your female friends nurture and support you, and how can you offer more of the same to them?

4. What is being mirrored to you in the relationships you are uncomfortable in?

5. What does commitment mean to you?

6. What are your beliefs about marriage?

7. Are you in any relationship where it is time to leave, and what work still needs to be done before you do?

8. What's the most important thing you've learned about relationship?

BB4

READER/CUSTOMER CARE SURVEY

We care about your opinions. Please take a moment to fill out this Reader Survey card and mail it back to us.
As a special **"thank you"** we'll send you exciting news about interesting books and a valuable **Gift Certificate.**

Please PRINT using ALL CAPS

First Name ______________ MI. ______ Last Name ______________

Address ______________________ City ______________

ST ______ Zip __________ Email: ______________

Phone # (____) ______________ Fax # (____) ______________

(1) Gender:

______Female ______Male

(2) Age:

______12 or under ______40-59
______13-19 ______60+
______20-39

(3) What attracts you most to a book?

(Please rank 1-4 in order of preference.)

	1	2	3	4
3) Title	O	O	O	O
4) Cover Design	O	O	O	O
5) Author	O	O	O	O
6) Content	O	O	O	O

(7) Where do you usually buy books?

Please fill in your top ***TWO*** *choices.*

1)______Bookstore
2)______Religious Bookstore
3)______Online
4)______Book Club/Mail Order
5)______Price Club (Costco, Sam's Club, etc.)
6)______Retail Store (Target, Wal-Mart, etc.)

Comments:

____
____
____
____
____
____

5

Making Choices

◆

Our minds are more than linear logic.
When we inform our logic with our feelings,
our intuition, our being, and our spirituality,
we're clearer and stronger.

—*Anne Wilson Schaef,* Words of Wisdom
for Women Who Do Too Much

MAKING *the* RIGHT CHOICE

When considering choices in your life, the "most alive choice" feels like a bit of a risk, makes you giggle, or makes the hairs at the back of your neck stand up.

—SARK, *THE BODACIOUS BOOK OF SUCCULENCE*

- Trusting my intuition is paramount. And if that voice is whispering too softly for me to hear it clearly, the key is to wait or postpone until the voice is stronger. If the circumstances do not allow either of these measures, I go for happiness, comfort, ease or adventure!

  —Maggie Argiro, home economist & writer

- Always make a decision based on what you know to be right—even if it means that it will be to your detriment financially, or cause you disappointment or discomfort.

  —Christina Bokelman, sign language interpreter

- I am learning that if I just go on accepting the framework for life that others have given me, if I fail to make my own choices, the reason for my life will be missing. I will be unable to recognize that which I have the power to change.

  —*Liv Ullmann, actress*

- Choice is easier when we realize that a higher power is actually making the choice. It's a question of then practicing listening or hearing what the higher power has to say.

  —*Nancy Leahy, mother & nature lover*

- Happiness is an inside job. Life is too short not to be happy. We make that choice every minute of every day. Do I feel good enough in this misery, or do I want something different? I'd rather be happy than right!

  —*Carol Richter, spiritual counselor*

When we ask for advice, we're usually not yet willing to accept the answers we already have within ourselves.

—ANNE WILSON SCHAEF, *WORDS OF WISDOM FOR WOMEN WHO DO TOO MUCH*

PEER PRESSURE

Think wrongly, if you please, but in all cases think for yourself.

—DORIS LESSING, AUTHOR

- Many of us have done things in our lives because someone else suggested it or pressured us to, or maybe it just looked like a cool thing to do. If you are feeling cool because you are using, your sense of knowing who you are has become confused with that feeling of coolness. You are something far deeper and greater than any feeling, emotion, or substance. . . . When you die, you die alone and you don't take coolness with you.

  —Wind Hughes, Daughters of the Moon, Sisters of the Sun

- You need to listen to your inner voice when something feels wrong, and exercise your choice to walk away from those situations. Empower yourself, resist peer pressure and do what is right for you. The true value of life is in living it fully.

  —Sandra-Leigh Serio, astrologer

- What is true for your friend may not be true for you. Each of us is learning our own unique set of personal lessons. You both may be facing challenges in your relationships, however your friend may be learning how to become more assertive while you're learning how to yield to others. When you are faced with a difficult situation, ask yourself, "What lesson am I now in the process of learning?" Stay on *your* course, and you will move through your life's path with greater ease.

  —Sheryll Hirschberger, therapist, writer & Feng Shui consultant

- Even though your teens are the time of the greatest peer pressure, I don't believe it ever really stops being a challenge. It's triggered by comparing. The joke is that everyone you're comparing yourself to is probably doing the same thing. It's the ones that are just themselves that everyone else really aspires to be like, wanting to be that *at home.*

  —Jenn Holden, social worker

◆

It feels vulnerable to trust your own voice, especially when it doesn't seem to match the popular trend, and yet this is where you step out of the mold and into your own power.

—DONNA BAASE, COSMETIC BUSINESS OWNER, ESTHETICIAN & EDUCATOR

Don't get caught up in the moment and let people make decisions for you under pressure. In our business I had a woman yell at me on the phone as I was trying to reconcile a mistake in her order. I buckled under the pressure and made a dumb choice I never would have in a clear moment. I practically gave away the ranch. I could have just said, "I will talk this over and will call you back." Step back, breathe and get back to where you have a more balanced perspective.

—Alexis Mayne, president, natural cosmetics company

MAKING MISTAKES

A mistake is simply another way of doing things.

—Katherine Graham, publisher

- All of us have been conditioned through schooling to believe that making mistakes is wrong. We received a failing grade for the wrong answer, so we spend the rest of our lives trying to avoid mistakes at all costs. And we pay for this with our fire and our creativity.

  —Justine Willis Toms & Michael Toms, TRUE WORK

- If life teaches us anything, it may be that it's necessary to suffer some defeats. Look at a diamond: It is the result of extreme pressure. Less pressure it is a crystal; and less than that it is fossilized leaves or just plain dirt.

  —Maya Angelou, LITTLE BIG BOOK OF LIFE

- Everyone makes mistakes. You are going to make mistakes. It is part of being human. Being young is a time of exploration. When you give yourself permission to make mistakes, you can experience more freedom to learn and grow and find out what you're made of.

—Barbara Foster, artist & Vedic astrologer

- Every mistake in my life has turned into a treasure. At the time I didn't realize it. When you connect with your deepest level of longing and let it take you where it wants, then even if it seems like the biggest mistake in the world, it will ultimately take you to your goal.

  —Farida Sharan, natural physician

- Wisdom starts with mistakes.

  —Anne Wilson Schaef, Native Wisdom for White Minds

- And the trouble is, if you don't risk anything, you risk even more.

  —Erica Jong, American writer & feminist

Think like a queen. A queen is not afraid to fail.
Failure is another stepping-stone to greatness.

—OPRAH WINFREY, TELEVISION TALK SHOW HOST

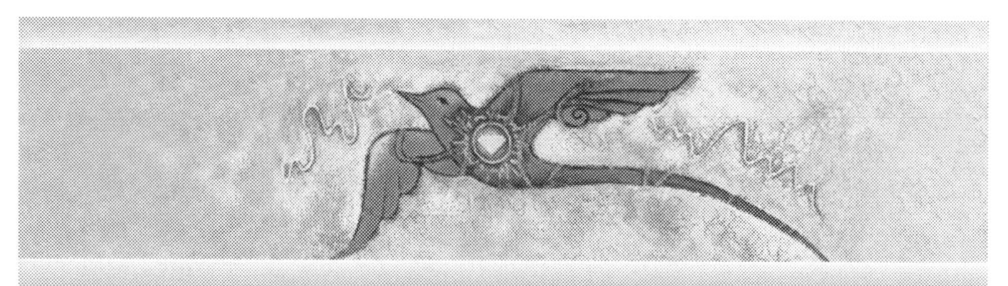

The DIAMOND MINE:
What would you have done differently in your life?

- I would have learned to hug in my early adult life, rather than waiting to trust others after the age of thirty.

—Name withheld

- The greatest regret of my life is not to have known my mother more intimately, to have discovered through more intimate communication and experience who she really was. I wish I had been more in touch consciously with her challenges, her joys, her heartbreaks as a woman.

—Rosemary Lucente, massage therapist

- My parents didn't have a lot of money, so I stole things when I was young. I hated that about myself, and I felt that I had to make it back up to God.

That has made me incredibly honest! I can't get away with anything. I try to really give back to the community.

—Marsha Wright, marketing account executive

- I wouldn't have slept with a lot of guys. I did, and I picked up an STD. You can pick one up and not even know it.

  —Name withheld

- I got married fairly young. And I think I would have been better off staying unmarried longer, having a little more time by myself without a partner, or husband, getting to know myself a little better, and then bringing more to a relationship.

  —DH, business & family manager

- I would have asked the question: *Is that true?* about myself much sooner, whenever someone said something negative to me or about me. I never considered the possibility that someone else was seeing things through their glasses.

  —Sheila Ross, mother, wife & community leader

- The one thing I am sorry I never did was something like Outward Bound. I think this is a really great way to build some skills in nature, with other people, facing your fears and being successful in very creative ways.

  —Name withheld

- I became a "caretaker" at a very young age and didn't learn to listen to my own needs and feelings. I wish I had had more balance there. You don't have to "do" a whole lot of things for people in order for them to like you. If you're just yourself people will like you. You don't have to win them over.

  — Mitzi Nicoletti, massage therapist & health care practitioner

- I would have put more time into scholastic activities. There's an unfulfilled scholar in me. I had a lot of issues . . . I was the only black child in most of my classes in a very white city, and there were not a lot of strong role models. My family was working class, and not many people we knew were college educated. Although I went to college, I was intimidated. I did well in my graduate master's program, but I wish I had been more courageous about stepping into scholarship and research.

  —Yaniyah Pearson, youth leadership director

- The thing I wish someone had said to me when I was twenty-eight, working at a job completely stressed out and anxious is: You don't have to suffer. It's just a job. You can experiment, try new things and not end up on the street if you take three months off. It should be a time of experimentation and travel so you can figure out who you are, so that then you'll know what you're supposed to do.

  —Arielle Ford, media relations expert & author

- I have several degrees, not because I wanted them to look good on my resume, but because I love to learn new things. But I am seeing more and more that following your internal guidance is a greater form of learning. I wish I had had more personal experiences and less reading about other people's experiences and truths.

—Lori Schreier, attorney, mediator & facilitator

- Nothing!

—Wanda Roth, fashion & jewelry consultant

- Just about everything!

—Shane Orne, riding coach & mother

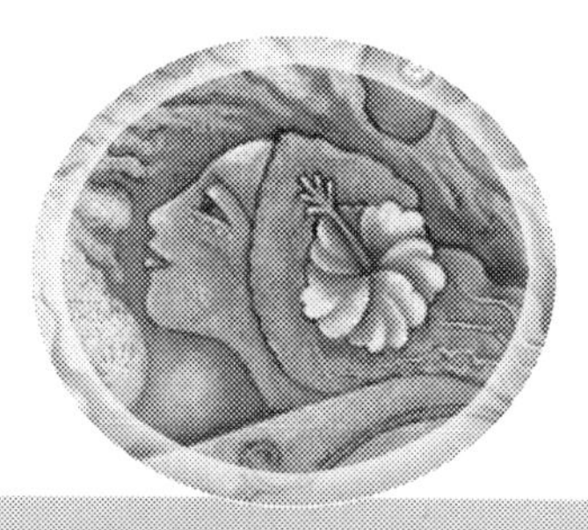

STEPPING-STONES *for* MAKING CHOICES

- We are usually not as trapped in a yes-no, win-lose situation as we think. Start with the seed choices and see if there are in fact more options. Put it on a huge piece of paper, writing down choices and repercussions, and let it play out in words, ideas and pictures. Just play in the moment, even be chaotic if that is the need. Then you can step back and see what is right under your nose.

  —Wendy Bramlett, yoga teacher & studio owner

- Flip a coin. If you're not happy with what comes up, do the opposite. You knew the answer all along.

  —Diana Wald, artist & general contractor

- Sit where you will be undisturbed. Go inside and ask for assistance by posing the question, "What would be for the highest good right now for all involved?" Listen for the answer and wait for the feeling of knowing. If it isn't clear, it may be that you might not want to listen. Remember what it has felt like in the past to receive a clear answer, and wait for that same sense of clarity.

  —Marlena Long, M.D.

- Sharing decision making with others is a great help, especially if you have difficulty making up your own mind. Being able to share decision making with your spouse, and sometimes including children in this process, not only helps get other viewpoints in the decision making, but also helps to build stronger relationships.

  —Heather Sanders, educator, wife & mother

- Use the Ben Franklin technique. Make a list with the pros on one side and the cons on the other. Then add it all up and see which has the highest score. If you have ten on one side and five on the other, then it's clear.

  —Marsha Wright, marketing account executive

- I remove myself mentally from the situation, pretend I'm a third party like a social worker or psychiatrist. That way, I can see the situation with fewer emotional ties to it—I can view it from the outside looking in.

  —Christine Bokelman, sign language interpreter

- Making choices has never come easy to me, so I pray a lot. I didn't always know that was available to me, even though I went to church all my life. But I do it now for small as well as big decisions. I know I have the answer when it's a gut feeling.

  —Maureen Read, seniors tennis player

- For me, the most practical way to make choices is to totally disengage the intellect. I imagine myself in one situation, for example, going to a movie with my friends. Then I ask myself how my heart feels. Next I imagine myself in the other situation, for example, staying home and finishing a really good book—and again I notice how my heart feels. Then I go with the choice that makes my heart feel better. Give yourself thirty seconds in each situation, imagining each scenario—put yourself there!

  —Amsheva Mallani, healer & teacher

- I am a slow decision maker. I think about things for a long time. I can really get things churned up agonizing over choices. My husband is really capable of seeing the big picture from his experience managing projects that take over five years to complete. I ask him for perspective. I also call on my mother, who is a very wise woman, and my closest friend, who has very deep understanding through her religious devotion. Having a few people you can trust and call upon for insight adds to your own perspective and gut instincts.

  —Donna Baase, cosmetic business owner, esthetician & educator

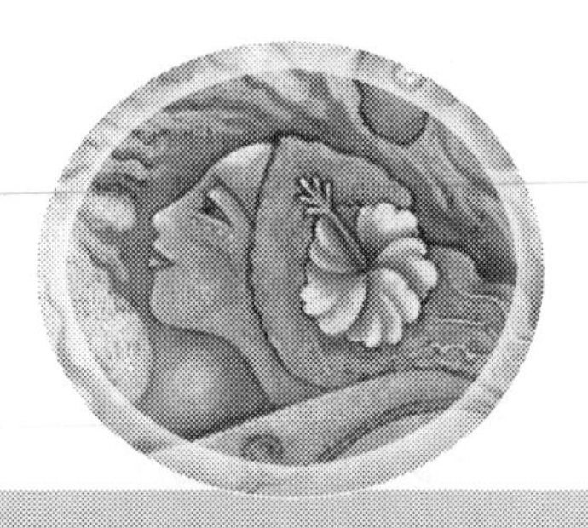

TURNING *your own* STONES

Get together with some girlfriends—in person or on-line—and ask yourselves these questions. You might want to write down the answers first, then share them with each other.

1. What big decisions are up for you, and could any of the tools in this section help you?
2. How has peer pressure influenced you in the past, and what more subtle forms of peer pressure are still tugging at you?
3. What mistakes have you made that you haven't yet seen the gift or the learning in? What could those gifts be?
4. What would you have done differently in your life?

6

Creating Your Destiny

◆

Everything is just waiting to be made up by us!

—*SARK,* The Bodacious Book of Succulence

THE CREATIVE FORCE

The call is what goes on when the kids are in bed, the lists are all put aside, the telephone has been turned down, you have a cup of tea, your feet are up and something is still pulling at your soul . . .

—ELIZABETH ROBERTS, *THE POSSIBLE HUMAN*

- Creativity is birthed from the unknown. It is a moment-to-moment expression, the spontaneous spark of life that comes from within to move outward, to move my being, to move my love, to move my essence, my heart, my passion into the world. It's living in the moment with the unknown. The more you can live in the unknown, the greater the force of the creativity that floods you and inspires you and designs you.

  —Lilli Botchis, Ph.D., alchemical researcher & adviser

- My creative life doesn't take on a form in terms of painting or writing or something specific like a lot of people have. I have often been down on myself for that, thinking maybe I should get some kind of creative life going here. But now I feel my creativity is the force of my life, and I am living creatively every second.

—DH, business & family manager

- My sexuality and spirituality have always been lively, together, as one. Even when young, I sensed, *Oh, this must be like God.* It is the divine spark of creativity. Some of my most incredible art work happens when my body is enlivened and turned on. I think, *Wow, what am I going to do with this energy? This is creative energy. I'll create!*

  —Becca Ferry, sacred arts painter & collector

- Creativity does not live in the domain of concepts . . . it does not bow down to the mind. Creativity ushers forth directly from soul through the heart, transcending mind, speaking directly to the heart and soul of others in the universal language of soul.

  —Wendy Grace Danner, metaphysical teacher & counselor

◆

I think the creative process is about creating who I am. In other words, I create myself through my creation, through my creative activity.

—MAYUMI ODA, PAINTER

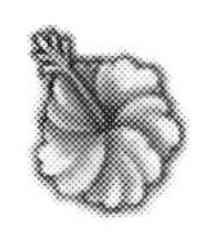

FINDING *your* PASSION

An aim in life is the only fortune worth finding.

—JACQUELINE KENNEDY ONASSIS

- What are you here for? Even asking this question may reveal the answer to you. And in knowing the answer, you're free to be who you are. So many women go about their lives and never even think about why they're here. They live, they die. I think we're all here for a reason, and we're here to touch others' lives.

  —Kay Newton, hotel sales & marketing director

- I think it's usually right in front of our eyes—that's why we miss it. Our society teaches us to only appreciate things we have achieved through effort and hard work. My learning has been to honor my gift of singing even though I thought, *Oh, anyone can do it . . . I just sing.* I eventually realized that it was a gift from God, and I am contributing something to the planet by honoring it. It's my way to share love.

  —Deva Premal, singer & musician

- I know what it's like to feel stuck, with nothing impassioning you. I have gone from one field of creative expression to another not knowing what I wanted to be or do. Just finding the little spark that turns you on and then following that to the fire will lead you step by step. Even if you open the door a crack just that one little spark will ignite your creativity. Trust and follow.

  —Prema Rose, former Broadway actress, filmmaker & midwife

- Let creativity fly! Have fun. Make your home *you*. Make your book great. Make your dance extraordinary. Have a good time. Be colorful. Dance wild. Sing out. Buy the dress you really want!

  —Sue Berkey, yoga teacher & mother

◆

Just don't give up trying to do what you really want to do.
Where there is love and inspiration, I don't think you can go wrong.

—ELLA FITZGERALD, SINGER

My passions found me—photography, music, concern and involvement in social and peace issues. I didn't seek any of these out, so it's hard to say anything about going out and finding your passion. If anything comes to you naturally, tickles your heart and lights a flame of interest in your mind, follow that magic impulse. For example, in high school my boyfriend handed me his camera and gave me a two-minute briefing on how to use it. The first role of film I took was magical, two little Arabian children on a playground. Within two weeks I was the assistant teacher in the photography class at Berkeley High School. I discovered that the camera was a natural extension of my body and my eye.

—Candace Freeland, photographer, musician & peace activist

ACTUALIZING *your* GIFTS

One can never consent to creep when one feels an impulse to soar.

—HELEN KELLER, SOCIAL ADVOCATE & REFORMER

- Our purpose, I believe, is not a thing, place, occupation, title, or even a talent. Our purpose is to be. Our purpose is *how* we live life, not what role we live. Our purpose is found each moment as we make choices to be who we really are.

  —*Carol Adrienne, The Purpose of Your Life*

- I knew as a young woman that I loved literature and wanted a career. The great fortune was that I never abandoned my dream despite difficulties, obstacles and the fact that it took a long time. Because I stuck with it, I have a lot to show for it in terms of doing what I love, earning a living and drawing a lot of recognition for it.

  —*Ellen Greene, classics professor*

- Knowing and following your passion is not for the fainthearted. I have lost my job, I've been sued, I was required to be tested right down to the depths of who I was, and in those tests, wondered if I was in the right profession and had the right passion. But true to what passion is, it stayed. It didn't get sidetracked.

  —Pamela George, Ph.D., professor & painter

- The worst slayer of creativity is this idea that it's outside you and there's some finished product you're supposed to produce. Just start from wherever you are, and anything that you are now doing can be a creative act.

  —Hilary Kurtz, publisher & editor

- A lot of people try to convince themselves that what they like to do is insufficient. If you like to quilt, and all your friends say, "But you have a master's degree," you should change your friends. I don't think it's so hard to know what you like to do. It's just hard to go against the flow.

  —Nikki Giovanni, political poet

◆

Life is to be lived. If you have to support yourself, you had bloody well better find some way that is going to be interesting. And you don't do that by sitting around wondering about yourself.

—KATHARINE HEPBURN, ACTRESS

PERSPECTIVES *on* EDUCATION

Live as if you were to die tomorrow. Learn as if you were to live forever.

—MAHATMA GANDHI

- I always keep myself in a position of being a student.

  —Jackie Joyner-Kersee, Olympic gold medalist

- I'm tired of playing worn-out depressing ladies in frayed bathrobes. I'm going to get a new hairdo and look terrific and go back to school and even if nobody notices, I'm going to be the most self-fulfilled lady on the block.

  —Joanne Woodward, actress

- Thinking for yourself is something we must bring to education. We women need to pass that belief on to younger generations!

  —Odetta, singer

- After a lot of education and several degrees, I still ask myself how it is that I want to live my life. Career goals can be met by pursuing a variety of paths, and education comes in many guises. Pursuing advanced degrees can be a brutal undertaking. Keep your humanity through the process.

—Andrea Girman, women's health practitioner & pediatrician

- I've always been glad that I worked hard and paid attention in school. With all the other issues to contend with in the business world, at least I did not have to worry about my knowledge as that was solid and something I could rely on.

  —Linda Elliott, former executive vice president, Visa

- A BMW can't take you as far as a diploma.

  —Joyce A. Myers, business executive

◆

E*ducation is what remains after one has forgotten everything one learned in school.*

—ALBERT EINSTEIN, PHYSICIST

DOING BUSINESS DIFFERENTLY

My idea of success is having time for deep rest, rejuvenation and self-discovery.

—FARIDA SHARAN, NATURAL PHYSICIAN

- The medals don't mean anything and the glory doesn't last. It's all about your happiness. The rewards are going to come, but my happiness is just loving the sport and having fun performing.

  —Jackie Joyner Kersee, Olympic gold medalist athlete

- A lot of young girls have looked to their career paths and have said they'd like to be chief. There's been a change in the limits people see.

  —Wilma Mankiller, first woman chief of the Cherokee Nations

- I do only the things I love to do. If I have a choice between doing A or B, I do what I love the most. I couldn't be a regular psychiatrist in a regular practice, making money, taking notes—it would drive me crazy! I couldn't work in academic life any more because of the baloney and academic-nonsense. I love to do my brand of medicine, just as I used to do as a country doctor. I still make house calls, here in the valley, and visit old, dying, and sick people. I love that. I'll always be a country doctor in my heart.

—Dr. Elisabeth Kubler-Ross in Tying Rocks to Clouds, *William Elliott*

- I will not teach or lecture anywhere in the world unless they let me lead them in dance first to release fear. Once that energy gets released, people and the whole room feel different—there's more freedom, openness and relaxation.

  —Farida Sharan, natural physician

- My business partner and I are owners of 400 acres of crystal mines in western Colorado. Sometimes the CEOs of companies don't know their workers, but we feel it's important. We visit with the miners at the mines. We take lunch to them and talk about our strategies and plan. The result is teamwork, and that they feel free to tell us anything, give us any kind of input.

  —Laurel Conrard, business owner

◆

The new worldview is emerging all over the planet . . . it can be seen in the growing interest in bringing spirituality into business and leadership.

—CAROL ADRIENNE, *THE PURPOSE OF YOUR LIFE*

I recently completed a fellowship in an emerging field of Western medicine called integrative medicine. At its most basic level, this field seeks to meld the best of complementary and alternative therapies with the best of mainstream medicine. It views the patient as a whole person in her/his own individual environment. This approach acknowledges the critical nature of the physician-patient relationship, advocates spending ample time getting to know each patient in order to empower her/him in making health-care choices, and draws upon the skills of a diverse team of health-care professionals and healers in order to provide the best medical care. This is medicine at its yummiest—co-creating an approach that is most in tune with the individual.

—Andrea Girman, women's health practitioner & pediatrician

MONEY & PROSPERITY

Life begets life. Energy creates energy.
It is by spending oneself that one becomes rich.

—SARAH BERNHARDT, FRENCH ACTRESS

- Make friends with money: Find joyfull ways to play with money. Stop speaking negatively about it. Encourage gratefulness for whatever you have. Magnify positive money feelings . . . money is fascinating, fun, mysterious and invigorating.

  —SARK, Succulent Wild Woman

- There is a great deal of difference between earning a great deal of money and being rich.

  —Marlene Dietrich, actress

- Prosperity is having the power to create a life of your choice—to get what you really want, not just what you're handed.

  —Ruth Ross, writer

- My parents taught me never to go in debt. As a result, debt is a stress I've never carried. It's an important lesson, especially in this culture, where it's so easy to get credit cards. Learn to budget your life. As your ability to make money grows, stay balanced.
  —Sue Berkey, yoga teacher & mother

- Becoming a professional was at first about financial independence from men and having freedom of choice. But now, having what I consider prosperity, I have had to look deeper into what I really care about. Prosperity is using the valuable time you have to do the things you want, and part of that is looking deeply into why you're here.
  —Lori Schreier, attorney, mediator & facilitator

◆

T*o fulfill a dream, to be allowed to sweat over lonely labor, to be given the chance to create, is the meat and potatoes of life. The money is the gravy.*

—BETTE DAVIS, ACTRESS

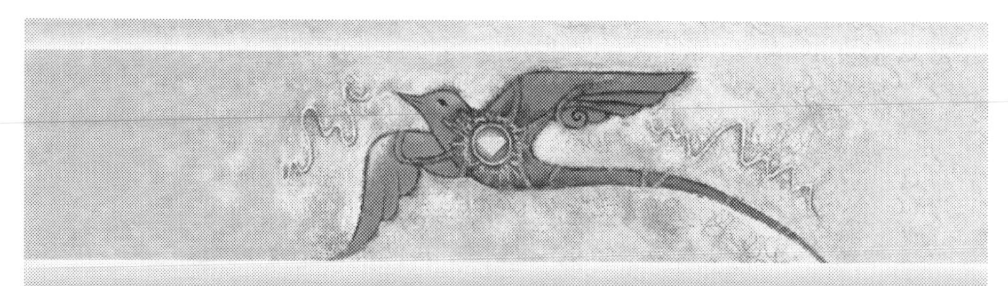

The DIAMOND MINE:
What are you grateful for that you did earlier in your life?

- When I was a child I took swim lessons. I had butterflies in my tummy all the way on the bus to my lessons. The excitement of being in the water led me to forty-two years of teaching and coaching swimming. Because of my love for swimming, I have been able to assist many people to swim with dolphins in the wild. It was significant, those early feelings deep inside me, connecting me to my path of service.

—Peggy Watson, retired self-esteem teacher & swim coach

- I joined the Peace Corps right out of college and spent two of the best years of my life teaching English in West Africa. Then I traveled around the world for a year before returning to the States. So many people have told me how they wish they had traveled when they were younger—once you head down the track of family and career, it's almost impossible to have that kind of adventure.

—JRH

- When I was fourteen I became a spiritual seeker, a product of Southern California's 1960s' flower-child awareness. Against the tide of parental disapproval I plunged into TM, yoga, vegetarianism and all things related with a youthful zeal. The significance has been a lifelong passion of putting inner peace and personal development above everything else in my life.

  —Jan Seehusen, mother & designer

- I'm really glad that I had my children when I was young. When my daughter was eighteen and moved away from home, I also moved, right into a new phase of my womanhood. We are very good "women" friends now, and I'm thankful to have had her and my son early.

  —Becca Ferry, sacred arts painter & collector

- I'm so glad I waited until I was thirty to have my first child. It gave me almost nine years after college to really sample what life is about, find my own place and my own journey, and then, by the time I had children, I was so, so thrilled to have them that it was just wonderful.

  —DH, business & family manager

- I was twenty-eight when I had my first child. Before that I became a computer engineer and worked on a design team. As soon as I had my first child, I stopped working outside the home. But it didn't matter. The fact was, I had had a career and was good at it. Just knowing that has been good for me all through my life. When I started having kids, I never stopped and thought, *Well, I wonder if I could have, I wonder if I would have,* because I knew I had.

— Sue Huggins, full-time mother

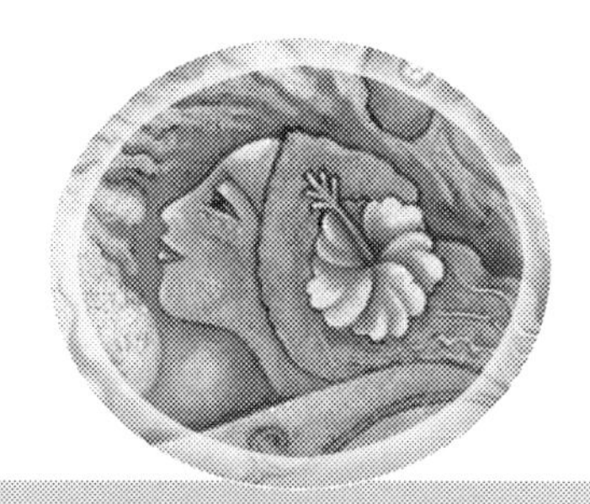

STEPPING-STONES *for* CREATING *your* DESTINY

- Find what you love and are excited about, and then surround yourself with people in that field who are doing it really well and whom you admire. I have phoned people and let them know that I am interested in what they are doing. I let them know that I have heard they were the best in the field or that I admire how they are doing it. They have been delighted to become my mentor. People are usually receptive to meeting with you and supporting you.

  —Mitzi Nicoletti, massage therapist & health care practitioner

- Write down the top ten or fifteen things that bring you joy. You'll see there is a thread that connects these things, a theme that reflects what you were born to do. Then take one step in that direction. It's a trap to think that you're going to be instantly in the perfect job. Figure out the most likely way to get there, and that's where you start.

—Marci Shimoff, professional speaker & author

- If the venue of your work doesn't matter, I think it's important to do it in *public* schools, universities, lands, housing, parks, libraries—because it matters to the world.

  —Pamela George, Ph.D., professor & painter

- Listen to the dreams you have at night. A lot of my direction has come to me in dreams, sometimes cryptic and symbolic, sometimes glaring and clear about what to do and how to find the answer. If I'm not listening, the dream repeats itself.

  —Arielle Ford, media relations expert & author

- Study what you love and everything else will flow. I chose chemistry as my major because I was really adept in math and science, and that's what I was being groomed for. I had a great deal of angst about changing my major to English and writing because, as a career, it isn't assumed to be the most lucrative. But, I did change and I loved it and so many doors have opened in response. When you are in the flow of your own heart you catch the wave of support from the universe.

  —Mary Capone, author, sound & movement teacher

- Any path you're on is the right path. I will never be a neurosurgeon; I was meant to be a divorce lawyer. It's not just what gets you excited. It's what you're built to do, and doing it in a way that you're not attached to it. To find out what it is, ask *What have I always been good at doing?* For example, if you like to watch television and figure out the plot, maybe you're meant to be a screenwriter.

  —Beth VanArsdale Krier, divorce attorney

- If I could have my wish for young women, I would have them craft their own creative lifestyles and not subject them to the workplace. With relentless work hours and striving for money, their creativity can be abused and they can be driven against their own cycles and feeling, sacrificed on the altar of today's business world. I would have them make their own hours and do what they love.

  —Farida Sharan, natural physician

- A lot of jobs appear to be very attractive and romantic until you are actually doing them. For instance, in midwifery there are a lot of things that I found very difficult and unattractive. I also had difficulty finding any personal balance. If I had had a more complete picture of my field before entering it, I would have known it wasn't a perfect match for me, and I might have chosen differently.

  —Terra Rafael, midwife & Ayurvedic practitioner

- Learn to enjoy spending time alone. Daydream. Investigate. Be bold! Experiment with abandon and the wonder of a child. Remember there is a use for everything, every skill, every gift. Ask yourself, "What if . . .?" "How does . . .?" etc.

  —Linda de Graaff, wife, mother & teacher

- Ask yourself: *What do I want most of all?* Then give everything you've got to it. Don't hold back at all. And be willing to take the consequences. If eventually it turns out that you realize that wasn't what you wanted, be willing to let it go. But until then, let it have you—all of you.

  —Nancy Cook, therapist

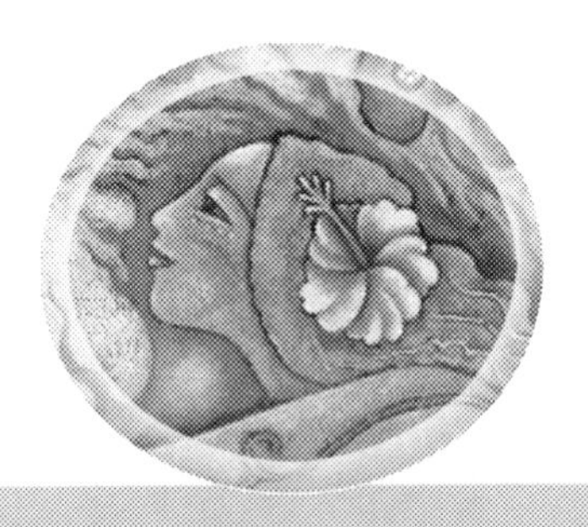

TURNING *your own* STONES

Get together with some girlfriends—in person or on-line—and ask yourselves these questions. You might want to write down the answers first, then share them with each other.

1. What are you here for? (Ask your heart, then write it down).
2. If you could create your own perfect working/creating/playing/resting day, how would it go?
3. What are your beliefs about money and prosperity? What would you like to believe?
4. What are you most passionate about, even if it's only a spark?
5. What are you grateful for that you did earlier in your life?

7

Finding Your Tribe

◆

Nobody, but nobody
can make it out here alone.

—Maya Angelou, poet, writer & educator

WOMEN'S GROUPS

Call it a clan, call it a network, call it a tribe, call it a family. Whatever you call it, whoever you are, you need one.

—JANE HOWARD, AUTHOR & JOURNALIST

- One of the most powerful tools for growth and honoring oneself is to gather together with other women with the intent to be with one another and to hear what others have to say about what's pressing on their hearts. When I meet regularly with my women's group, I come out strengthened, powerful, grateful. It feeds my spirit, makes me feel healthy and powerful, and I learn so much about myself. It's good medicine, girl medicine.

  —*Catherine Carter, health educator*

- If we can connect in groups, by phone or e-mail, at bookstores, churches and teahouses, if we can share our creative spirit with other women, we will bloom and ripen and grow.

  —*SARK, Succulent Wild Woman*

- When I visited my grandmother's village in Italy I was surrounded by a group of women who would come together to do their work—snapping beans, sewing, etc. We would laugh and touch, support each others' strengths and kid about each others' personalities. It was so sweet and nurturing. When we would return from church as a tribe of women singing "Ave Maria" down the stone street, there was nowhere else, I was at home.

  —Mary Capone, author, sound & movement teacher

◆

This is our way as women—to sit in circle. Our culture is just now recognizing this. This is natural and essential. It's not a tag on; it's the fabric of our being whole.

—MELISSA MICHAELS, SOCIAL ARTIST & EDUCATOR

My most profound experience was with a group that supported a member in the last weeks of her life. We would sit with her, gently touching her head or shoulder or foot, or singing sweet songs or lullabies. I remember her deep gratitude, and having her look into my eyes and call me her sister. For me, as an only child, that was truly a moment that I will treasure forever.

—Candace Freeland, photographer,
musician & peace activist

SPIRITUAL FAMILIES

When indeed shall we learn that we are all related one to the other, that we are all members of one body?

—HELEN KELLER, SOCIAL REFORMER & ADVOCATE

- Each of us is born into a biological family. Whether you stay in connection and love with them or not, you will find others along the way that resonate with you, and support and enhance your present values and goals. These people become your "spiritual family."

  —J&B

- Our society is not structured around community, but where there are pockets of it, life is so much richer and easier. It's utterly necessary, the direction we have to go in. The idea that we can function without each other is simply not true.

  —SP, mother of many

- I don't think of myself as an individual ever. I'm part of an extended group. So whatever happens to me happens to the group. If I make a better living and more money, the whole group goes with me. And if I'm ever impoverished, I will always find refuge in that group. So, you give a lot and you receive a lot. That's the way I visualize life—as a village. It takes a village to survive.

  —*Isabel Allende, On Women Turning 50*

- We need each other to spark each other, prime each other, hone each other. That is why every great spiritual form that enters into the world always gathers around it an ashram, or a community, or a sangha. It needn't be a formal kind of community; it can be just a community of a few friends who gather together regularly at a sacred time and place. . . .

  —*Jean Houston, Tying Rocks to Clouds, William Elliott*

◆

Community is not something we can "make" happen. Community emerges as we participate in life with those around us.

—ANNE WILSON SCHAEF, *NATIVE WISDOM FOR WHITE MINDS*

MENTORS

Surround yourself with people who are going to lift you higher.
—OPRAH WINFREY, TELEVISION TALK SHOW HOST

- I had great mentors, aunts and grandmothers. They were always working hard and enjoying what they were doing. I even had a good mentor at McDonald's. She had one arm, and she swept the floor so lovingly, with such a beautiful stroke that it made tears come to my eyes. There are mentors everywhere
—Shar Lee, yoga teacher & cranial therapist

- Observe older women—who do you want to be like? What is it about a woman that makes you want to hug her and touch her? Find an intangible quality about her and make it yours. *—Rosie Estrin, healer & counselor*

- For a mentor I want someone who can see me for real. Someone who sees through my cleverness and masks and understands me. She guides me from a place of wisdom and unconditional love, like a fairy godmother.

—Sage Hamilton, community leader & women's group facilitator

- Look for the people who inspire you and don't be afraid to ask and pursue. Trust that life is good and there is support if you seek it and are open to it.

  —Ulla Hoff, yoga teacher & counselor

- When you are isolated and going through trials and difficulties, a mentor's feedback and support are very necessary. I was so wrapped up in my head that I didn't understand it was okay to have needs and feelings. Let your feelings have a voice, communicate what you need to an older woman. It is scary to trust that you will be loved and accepted—but it is scarier to stay isolated and unexpressed.

  —Name withheld

◆

And remember, we all stumble, every one of us.
That's why it's a comfort to go hand in hand.

—E. K. BROUGH, AMERICAN WRITER

I would have spent more time with my parents and grandparents. Now that I am a septuagenarian, I understand that many memories are not so much remembering what they said or did but rather how we felt just being with them—just watching the way they moved with the light of dawn on their faces, and the way they carried themselves when they were tired from the work of the day and still had work to do. I wish I had studied that. I believe there is much to be learned from folks in our bloodline in their simple gestures and what gave them strength and what allowed them to endure.

—Peggy Watson, dolphin facilitator & swim coach

YOU BELONG

If we have no peace, it is because we have forgotten we belong to one another.

—MOTHER TERESA, HUMANITARIAN

- You know, with one person, it's hard to see very far. Two people you can see a little more. But if you have a whole group of people around really caring about you and telling you, "You are doing the right thing! We want you to be around! Give us your gifts!" it helps you fulfill your purpose.

  —*Aobonju Sobonfu Somé,* THE SPIRIT OF INTIMACY

- You are never a burden to members of your tribe—you deserve to be nourished by other women and community.

  —*J&B*

- Nothing is itself without everything else. Community is a practice field where we get to practice the art of inclusion. We learn to bow to the whole by practicing the same devotion we would give an esteemed teacher. The community is our teacher. If we can practice that way, then awareness and enlightenment come from our community.

—Mukara Meredith, leadership consultant & community educator

- Vulnerability is a shortcut to self-acceptance. When you share the truth of your inner reality with other women, you find out that you are not an isolated case, but a piece of the larger whole of womanhood.

—Sheila Ross, mother, wife & community leader

◆

You don't have to worry about finding your tribe—they will find you! Look at the people in your life now. Lean on your allies and walk away from those who are not.

—J & B

No matter what culture you come from, if you push our lineage back far enough, you get a whole assortment of short people sitting around a fire telling stories! . . . We have the sense of having done this before, of being accomplished at it. And perhaps millennia ago, they felt very accomplished at this also. But what they knew that we are just starting to discover is that the stories are absolutely indispensable for the collective, for the tribe to continue, and for the individual to prosper as well as the collective. We're just starting to discover the importance of sharing those stories in a circle and having people bear witness.

—Charles Garfield, coauthor, WISDOM CIRCLES,
in an interview with NEW DIMENSIONS RADIO

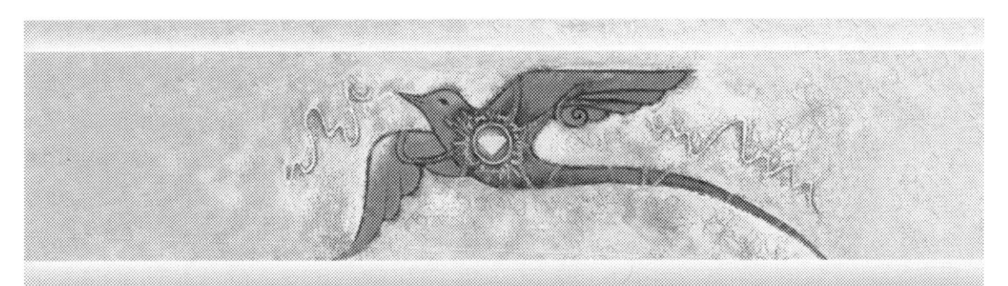

The DIAMOND MINE:
What has been your experience with women's groups?

- They should be a lifetime choice—join or create a women's group and never be without one. I've been in one for thirty years. We are involved in each other's lives and progress together, sharing our stories through all the phases that everybody goes through. The combined experience and wisdom is powerful! It's incredibly strengthening.

  —Sue Berkey, yoga teacher & mother

- One of the most valuable support systems I've had throughout my life has been my women's groups. I was in one group for twelve years and I am in two groups now. The greatest value has been having women who understand and honor my dreams, help me to see clearly the places where I have blind spots, and help me to stay moving in the flow and direction that I want my life to move in. We have been together through every kind of experience—marriage, divorce, children, death, career changes, moves. The fact that these women are always there with love and wisdom and clarity and care has been a great blessing.

—Marci Shimoff, professional speaker & author

- I don't belong to a women's group. I go through life with friends with whom I resonate, and who naturally appear around me. It is precious to interact and share with women, and I truly enjoy everyone as long as they are in my life; some even stay lifelong friends. But sometimes I have a wonderful conversation with a woman I never see again. We may connect deeply, even solve each other's heartache because we were completely truthful with each other in the moment.

—Emilie Taylor, wife, mother & strategic planner

- My favorite women's circle is two women who really trust each other. We see the best and highest in each other, we help each other, we love each other unconditionally, and it's easy to work through problems. She's a constant source of love and support to me. It's a very balanced, eye-to-eye friendship. I can be all that I am with her and she can be all that she is with me. We're also connected in our intuition, so we can see into each other's blind spots. No woman is ever perfect, and you have to be yourself fully with a true friend.

—Diane Frank, poet & novelist

- I think it's innate within us as women to gather together. One of the great gifts we have is that we're different from men. I treasure my circle of girlfriends with whom I've been close since college. They've helped support me in all the good times, to share all of life's experiences, and been an incredible support through the hard times. After my accident, one of my girlfriends came to my house every week for a whole year to take care of my personal business for me.

  —Kiki Corbin, naturopathic doctor & minister

- The most intentional one I did was in graduate school at Berkeley when I was learning how to be a therapist. We were exploring feminism, and we all got to talk about things frankly, about who we were as women, what our issues were and possible ways to resolve them. We were aware that we had feminine powers—intuition, nurturing, compassion—and we wanted to empower ourselves with them. We wanted to make a difference with our lives. None of us had previously dared to identify ourselves in that way, with a commitment to change our world.

  —Kim Antara Greene, psychotherapist & foundation director

- I've belonged to several different groups: quilting, a relationships support group, and parents of child athletes—the "bleacher warmers." I love the support that comes in getting a project done, and the sharing of knowledge about how to get something done. But I have especially loved the support in parenting that comes from sitting with a group of mothers at sports events and discovering our kids were, after all, perfectly normal!

—*Wendy Read, reconciliation analyst & fabric artist*

- For me, community is centered around church. I haven't belonged to a church since I was a child, but I go to a women's Sunday school group now. I love these women, and we take care of each other. We comfort in times of loss of a partner, and they checked in on Emily, my daughter, when I was away. Their obligation may have started with the Sunday school class, but that's only half an hour. The commitment extends far beyond that.

  —*Linda de Graaff, wife, mother & teacher*

- For the past six years I have been a member of a women's circle that meets on holy days (*sabbats*) and at other times to celebrate and honor events going on in our lives. We pray, meditate, dance, sing and drum. We honor spirit, the seasons, nature and any and everything we hold special. I use ancient and traditional forms of ritual, but I also create my own ceremonies. . . .

  —*Wind Hughes, Daughters of the Moon, Sisters of the Sun*

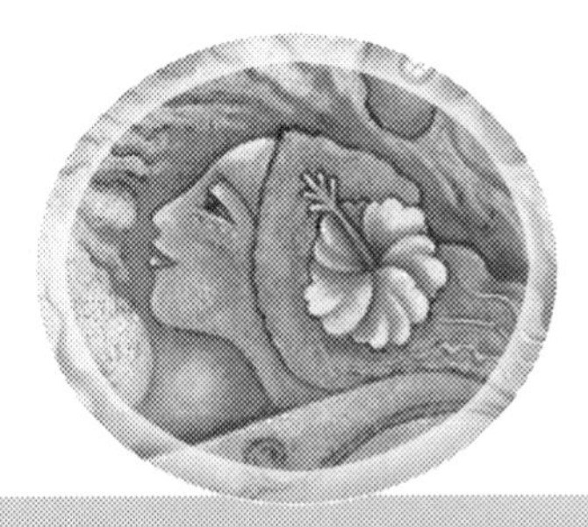

STEPPING-STONES *for* CREATING *a* WOMEN'S CIRCLE

- A women's group is a place to help us along and help us find our voice. It is a safe place outside the norms of society to be what we want to be. Find a room or a house, a space to be listened to and to listen, where you can compare, contrast, create, reinvent and essentially be yourself fully. It is a place to serve and be served into greatness.

  —Jennifer Garcia, seminar leader & women's group facilitator

- Just get together and allow for the truths to unfold. Make up what you do as you go along. Meet, move, dance, sing, do your hair and nails! You are coming together to generate energy and juice each other up. Create some central excuse or point of the gathering, but the main purpose is to generate trust and to gift each other rather than chatting or complaining. It will deepen over time with a commitment to meet.

—*Amy McCarrel, seminar leader & women's group facilitator*

- As a women's group facilitator I guide women in building community and supporting one another's lives. I also support them creatively expressing themselves. I use the mediums of expressive movement, drawing, painting, crafting, improvisation, role playing or whatever feels right for that group at that time. Through creative expression we loosen the grip we have on limited stories we have about ourselves and open to the possibility of living our lives differently, more fully and more openly.

—*Sage Hamilton, community leader & women's group facilitator*

- There is a three-fold purpose in coming together. First, you pause and reconnect with yourself. Second, you connect with other women. Third, you get in touch with the bigger story of why you are here, what you came to do. I do that through the creative process which, for me, is always body-centered. I always begin the circle with a warm up—something experiential because women metabolize life through the body.

—*Melissa Michaels, educator, social artist & mother*

- A women's circle is a wonderful technique for harnessing the natural power of the "whole" being greater than the sum of the parts. Gather women who share the following qualities: truthfulness, compassion, faith in a higher power, commitment to mutual growth and gratitude. You need a commitment to meeting regularly, and confidentiality. The more you meet, the more you'll expose yourself to the higher good.

  —Holly Moore, artist & mother

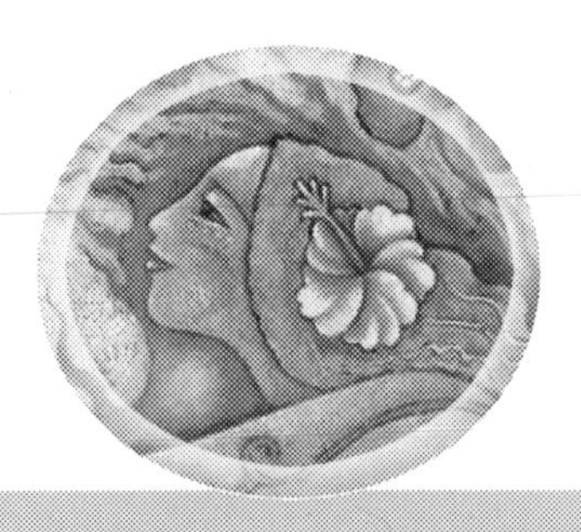

TURNING *your own* STONES

Get together with some girlfriends—in person or on-line—and ask yourselves these questions. You might want to write down the answers first, then share them with each other.

1. Who do you consider your support team? If you don't feel you have one, who would you ask to create one with you, and what would be the qualities you'd look for?
2. Who do you recognize as the mentors in your life—those whom you look to for inspiration and support?
3. What are some ideas for women's group activities you would like to be part of, or just some excuses for getting together with other women?
4. Start talking about the "diamonds, pearls & stones" in your life to other women in groups, chat rooms and wherever and whenever it moves you and makes you bigger.

8

Honoring Yourself

◆

I learned to take time for myself and to treat myself with a great deal of love and respect 'cause I like me . . . I think I'm kind of cool.

—Whoopi Goldberg, actress & comedienne

SPEAKING *your* TRUTH

We are volcanoes. When we women offer our experience as our truth, as human truth, all the maps change. There are new mountains.

—URSULA K. LE GUIN, AMERICAN WRITER

- In telling the truth about our lives, we can cleanse the infection and close the open, painful wounds that have distorted us, have kept us from realizing all that is possible for ourselves. And in sharing the truths, in opening our secrets together, our common wounds—women's wounds—may be healed.

  —Susan Wittig Albert, Ph.D., WRITING FROM LIFE

- Do not limit yourself so that other people can feel comfortable. It is natural to be social and be liked, but don't sell out. No one grows from mediocrity. People may be threatened or jealous, but allow for that discomfort—walk through the fire and stay in your truth. I have been told that I can walk into a room at times and my energy is so strong that it disturbs some people. Being a "caretaker," I have often held back to make people feel safe. But in the long run, people admire people who can stand firm in their truth.

—Mitzi Nicoletti, massage therapist & health-care practitioner

- If I'm too strong for some people, that's their problem.

  —Glenda Jackson, actress

- Feel your truth, speak your truth, live your truth—and your life will be an inspiration to all you touch. You will have the pearl of greatest value: inner peace—more precious, in my opinion, than a handsome, successful husband; glittering social life; dazzling career or perfect body; or whatever else you hope to attain.

  —Wendy Grace Danner, metaphysical teacher & counselor

◆

The truly free woman is one who knows
how to decline a dinner invitation without giving an excuse.

—ANONYMOUS

LISTENING *to your* INNER VOICE

And no one will listen to us until we listen to ourselves.
The Goddess awakens in our hearts before she awakens in the world.

—MARIANNE WILLIAMSON, *A WOMAN'S WORTH*

- Listening is a fabulous skill to develop. Listen to yourself, to other women and to your children. There are so many levels of listening. When you listen with your heart rather than your mind, you listen from a place of love, which is very accepting.

  —Mary Cave, life coach

- When you're presented with information, whether it involves other people's or society's values or information at school or work, there's a tendency just to accept it. Stop and go into your own silent inner chamber, and take note of whether that value, statement, or information makes common sense to you. Does it have truth for you?

  —Lilli Botchis, Ph.D., alchemical researcher & adviser

- Don't be afraid to amplify your inner voice. If you do, you'll hear the melody in your mind, feel the beat in your heart and the joy in your soul. Some days will feel like rock and roll. Others might be a Hallelujah chorus or a solo flute. But if you learn to listen, you'll also learn to dance with your spirit. Then every other partner or goal you choose will reflect both your inner voice and your emerging sense of grace.

—Helen Rosenau, the Internet's "Jewish fairy godmother"

◆

I'll walk where my own nature would be leading:
It vexes me to choose another guide.

—EMILY BRONTE, ENGLISH NOVELIST

After six years of marriage I realized that I had compromised myself by deferring to my husband's style of functioning. I asked myself why I often started things, then stopped—I realized that often it was because my husband asked questions I couldn't answer. I would take him a plan, for approval (not advice, but approval)—and he would point out all the reasons it wouldn't work. I was suffocating.

One day I simply had had enough and I just excused him from playing that role any more. We still run things by each other, and he's still my source of good business sense, but I no longer depend on what he thinks of a project, or whether he even understands it. The result is that the universe has been swooping in to support things. I rarely know how things will unfold—but I do it my way. I don't have a clue where the boat is going, but I've come to rely on my intuition. It usually heads me in the right direction.

—Stacey Hurlin, artist & community leader

SETTING BOUNDARIES

Don't compromise yourself. You are all you've got.

—JANIS JOPLIN, SINGER

- We need to find the courage to say "no" to the things and people that are not serving us if we want to rediscover ourselves and live in our authenticity.

  —*Barbara De Angelis, writer & speaker*

- The receptive feminine has been misinterpreted as "passive." So, we need to make conscious decisions about when to receive and when to shut the gate.

  —*Nina Boyd Krebs, CHANGING WOMAN, CHANGING WORK*

- If you want to be involved with a man, the first question to ask is: Does he deserve you? It's okay to say yes, but it's also okay to say no. And don't do anything that doesn't feel right to you. Live your life in terms of your own inner wisdom even if it's different from what people have been telling you, and especially if it's different from what people have been telling you.

—Diane Frank, poet & novelist

- Setting boundaries is not disrespectful, bad or wrong. In fact, boundaries make you feel SAFE in your environment and actually prevent you from being hurt. Personal boundaries are healthy, good for you. Setting boundaries raises your sense of self-worth, your self-esteem, because you are sending yourself the message that you are WORTHY of care.

—Coach Rinatta Paries in THE RELATIONSHIP COACH NEWSLETTER

♦

Protect yourself so that nobody overrides you, overrules you, or steps on you. You just say, "Just a minute, I'm worth everything, dear."

—MAYA ANGELOU, *DAUGHTERS OF THE MOON, SISTERS OF THE SUN*

BREAKING BOUNDARIES

Alice laughed: ". . . one can't believe impossible things."
"I dare say you haven't had much practice," said the Queen.
"When I was younger, I always did it for half an hour a day.
Why sometimes I've believed as many as
six impossible things before breakfast."

—LEWIS CARROLL, *ALICE IN WONDERLAND*

- You've got to rattle your cage door. You've got to let them know that you're in there, and that you want out. Make noise. Cause trouble. You may not win right away, but you'll have a lot more fun.

  —Florence Kennedy, actress

- The young do not know enough to be prudent, and therefore they attempt the impossible—and achieve it, generation after generation.

  —Pearl S. Buck, American writer

- I am willing to put myself through anything; temporary pain or discomfort means nothing to me as long as I can see that the experience will take me to a new level. I am interested in the unknown, and the only path to the unknown is through breaking barriers, an often painful process.

  —Diana Nyad, first woman to swim the English Channel

- I stand for freedom of expression, doing what you believe in and going after your dreams.

  —Madonna, singer

◆

I *don't go by the rule book—I lead from the heart, not the head.*

—DIANA, PRINCESS OF WALES

LIVING *for* OTHERS

You must love and care for yourself, because that's when the best comes out.

—TINA TURNER, SINGER

- One of the hardest things about being a woman in a busy world is that we tend to put ourselves last on the to-do list. Caught up in a culture of doers, we become what many writers, male and female, have labeled human doings, instead of human beings. While both genders can fall into the doing trap, women have a harder time getting out. . . . The big question becomes, "How can I get what I need without being selfish to others?" As long as we think that spending time on ourselves is selfish, the vicious jaws of the doing trap will stay locked around our ankles.

  —Joan Borysenko, A Woman's Journey to God

- The tremendous benefit of "women's liberation" has been that women feel empowered to do whatever they are capable of without societal restriction. However, a kind of pressure seems to have been created simultaneously that subliminally whispers, "You have to be all things to all people at all times." Why do women feel we have to justify our existence with motherhood, career, wifehood, creative expression, volunteerism, friendships and so many other hats being worn simultaneously?

—Jan Seehusen, mother & designer

- I feel I live for myself now, but when I was actively mothering, I lived for others—to my detriment, I think. I wish I had created a life outside my family. All I did was take care of my kids and husband, and it created a lack of balance. That was my whole purpose—and I can't say I was happy doing it. I just accepted the fact that society said that's what you do.

  —Nancy Leahy, mother & nature lover

- Pain—emotional or physical—is my barometer for knowing when I'm living too much for others. When I experience pain as a result of putting others first, I step back—psychically, physically, emotionally—and allow that person to be in his or her own soul-knowing. This puts me in my own soul-knowing. I immediately feel better, and joy comes through.

  —Jacquelina Davis, LMT & NIA instructor

◆

When I care for myself, then I can really be of service in this world. It's the oxygen theory on the airplane: we have to put on our own mask first before attending to the children.

—MARCI SHIMOFF, PROFESSIONAL SPEAKER & AUTHOR

CREATING BALANCE

For fast-acting relief try slowing down.
—LILY TOMLIN, ACTRESS & COMEDIENNE

- Balance is not about juggling. Modern woman juggles her life in a frantic attempt to do and be it all. Stop! Just stop a minute. Did you walk last night under the stars? Did you listen to the song of that bird? We cannot find balance when we ignore the beauty that is all around us. Beauty is what women are all about. Go inside and begin to wear that outside. However you access peace ultimately shows up in your balance.

  —Peggy Watson, dolphin facilitator & swim coach

- We do not have to get sick in order to get some rest. I think many diseases in women are a way of getting some rest time. It's the only excuse that many women will allow themselves in order to take time off. They have to be flat on their backs before they will say no.

  —Louise Hay, EMPOWERING WOMEN

- No one can tell you what balance means for you. Get out of the shoulds and comparisons. We are *supposed* to be wholeheartedly there in our relationships. We're *supposed* to be the primary caregivers to our children. We're *supposed* to create income, make brilliant meals and do all that really well. We expect it of ourselves and it is expected of us. But this is a Western idea. Visit other cultures and see how differently they view stress and achievement. We would rather have mediocrity in many different avenues than excellence in one or two.

—Wendy Bramlett, yoga teacher & studio owner

◆

The most important advice I can give a woman when it comes to juggling career and marriage is to put herself first. Selfish? Not at all. After all, whose life is it?

—DR. JOYCE BROTHERS, *THE SUCCESSFUL WOMAN*

This is a beautiful quote from the Zen text. I've put the gender a woman, but it could be applied to a man, too. "A woman who is the master of the art in living makes little distinction between her work and her play, her labor and her leisure, her mind and her body, her education and her recreation, her love and her religion. She hardly knows which is which. She simply pursues her vision of excellence and grace in whatever she does, leaving others to decide whether she is working or playing. To her she is always doing both."

—Lynne Twist, author, The Soul of Money, in an interview with New Dimensions Radio

HAVING FUN

Why not seize the pleasure at once? How often is happiness destroyed by preparation, foolish preparation?

—JANE AUSTEN, ENGLISH WRITER

- Too much of a good thing can be wonderful.

  —Mae West, actress

- If someone said, "Write a sentence about your life," I'd write, "I want to go outside and play."

  —Jenna Elfman, actress

- Risk exploring what terrifies you. Fun comes in many forms. Whatever opens you and allows you to locate a new source of strength that has been held back is thrilling. And you know exactly what that is. Play with it.

  —Jennifer Garcia, seminar leader & women's group facilitator

- When I was about nineteen, I heard a great teacher say, "Life is bliss and we are here to enjoy." When I heard this, I realized that I had submitted to a cultural paradigm that said, "Life is a struggle." Just hearing someone I trusted describe the joy and bliss in life allowed me to have more fun, not take life as seriously, and laugh.

  —Barbara Foster, artist & Vedic astrologer

- We don't have enough fun. Although there is much to cry about in this world, it's worth finding life's joy and focusing on life's beauty because they always exist in one form or another. Find something or someone to play with, often and full out.

  —Andrea Girman, women's health practitioner & pediatrician

◆

What a wonderful life I've had! I only wish I had realized it sooner.

—COLETTE, FRENCH WRITER

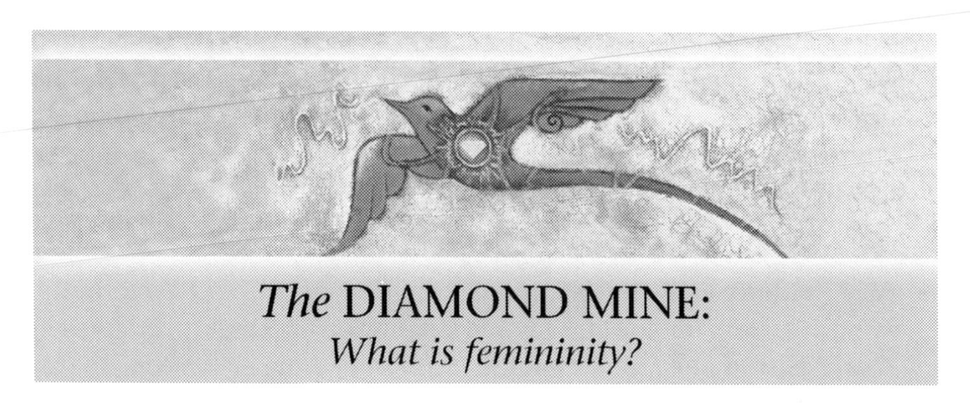

The DIAMOND MINE:
What is femininity?

- I have a knee-jerk reaction against the word because it has this stigma of ruffles and submission. I'd like to get rid of the word and replace it with what you've referred to in this book—authentic female power. That's what I'd like femininity to mean.

  —Holly Moore, artist & mother

- Being a woman is an elixir! If young women learn to listen to the calling of that elixir—because it is a high calling—there's nothing this world needs more. True Femininity will not be dissuaded. She knows who she is, she knows the contribution that being feminine makes, and she will neither downplay it herself or allow another to do so. The cost is too high personally and it's too high socially.

  —Glynda Yoder, business owner

- Femininity means being in touch with my more yin receptive female side, which reflects certain characteristics. I have both masculine and feminine, but my feminine nature is expressed as it is in women across cultures: it's receptive, creative, compassionate, intuitive, flowing, open, loving, wise and connected to all beings on the earth. And it's strong! But it's strong in a magnetic way, rather than a forceful way.

  —Marci Shimoff, professional speaker & author

- In the God force, there is structure and flow. Both are necessary. There must be the strength of something that can hold the form, but it has to have a flow. For me, femininity is that powerful flow that goes through structure.

  —Glynda Yoder, business owner

- Feeling feminine is about the way I hold my body. The way I carry it. The way it moves when I walk through time and space. It's kind of like a cosmic dance that's always changing and unfolding.

  —Jacquelina Davis, LMT & NIA instructor

- Femininity would look great in a gunny sack. It is not what you wear or how you are sexually, it is how you carry forth your connection to mother earth. It is the flow from within that honors the integration of male and female.

  —Peggy Watson, dolphin facilitator & swim coach

- There are many faces of the Goddess. Round, flowing, soft, receptive—or tight, closed and angry. Women walking from the base of their body. Silk, colors, flowers, beauty. A place of mystery. Nurturing. A little girl in a field dancing with fairies. It's all feminine.

  —Hope Robertson, artist & healer

- Femininity is earth mother, the prototypes of unconditional love and compassion, nurturing, the ability to stand in the fire with someone who's going through a lot and hold them. It's the connection between the intuitive divine and the expression of that in our lives.

  —Kim Antara Greene, psychotherapist & foundation director

- Femininity is the surrender into the vastness of life. It's the tides, the seasons, everything that has cycles—that's the feminine aspect of life to me.

  —Nancy Cook, therapist

- To say "divine feminine" is redundant.

  —Rachel Bagby, in CHANGING WOMAN, CHANGING WORK, Nina Boyd Krebs, Ed.D.

STEPPING-STONES *for* HONORING YOURSELF

- I finally decided to stop waiting for someone else to give me things, and started giving them to myself. For example, I started writing beautiful notes to other people, expressing the kind of heartfelt messages I would like to receive, and it made me feel I was fulfilling my own desire for that.

  —Catherine Carter, health educator

- My philosophy is very simple: when in doubt, take a bath.

  —Sarah Ban Breathnach, writer

- I like having a daily routine that supports my feeling good. That includes meditation, time for myself, exercise and dance, eating in a way where I feel healthy, spending time in nature and doing things that make my heart sing. Although I don't do everything every day, the more I listen to myself, the more I am guided to know what I need in any given moment.

—Marci Shimoff, professional speaker & author

- Solitude. I like to putz—it's like a meditation. I don't have a problem not seeing someone for forty-eight hours or more. I can let the phone ring! This way I fill my glass full again. Then I can relate to others.

  —Laurel Conrard, business owner

- My training is in vision quests, a ceremonial way of being alone on earth, but with your community back at base camp waiting for you. Being in community, spending a chunk of time on earth, is my favorite way of honoring myself. I also love traveling in certain third world countries like India or Peru, because if I spend time with people who are simpler and more on the earth, then my anxiety and tendency toward depression start dropping off.

  —Carol Parker, psychotherapist & wilderness guide

- My favorite way of taking care of myself is through dance, vocalization and music, especially drumming. I need to unleash my voice, let my voice just sing and express its deepest feelings, whether pain, joy, supplication to the divine, anger or love.

  —Candace Freeland, photographer, musician & peace activist

- When I come home from work, I take a bath and change my clothes so I can leave my work energy behind and step into my feminine energy. This way my husband can be the guy. Otherwise I'm still in work mode and still in masculine energy. Unless you're a massage therapist, it's hard to be in your feminine energy when you're working.

—Arielle Ford, media relations expert & author

- Doing yoga! It's like an internal massage, physically as well as energetically and spiritually. Yoga provides a metaphor for my life. When I get off center and go deep in yoga, everything falls back into place. The movements are almost incidental to breath. All the stuff I'm doing in my life is really incidental to breathing through life.

—Beth VanArsdale Krier, divorce attorney

- I try to take care of myself as much as I can, choosing a life that makes me feel whole. It's little things, very little things: showering, putting cream on the body, washing my hair, getting a massage, buying good organic food, taking supplements, caressing my partner in passing. Actually, the appreciation of all these things is a result of the integration of meditation in my life. For me it has to be the "whole life."

—Deva Premal, singer & musician

- Getting a massage, dancing, making love and giving myself unstructured time so that I can write poetry and novels. I love being on mountains and hiking and traveling to places I haven't been before, so the world is new. Music is very important to me. With the right music, I go into rapture, and I've been playing cello since I was ten years old.

  —Diane Frank, poet & novelist

- I love everything about being on the beach. I love doing yoga and meditating, which for me means just being quiet and listening. I love brushing my skin and hair in the morning. I love making vegetable juice. I love drinking water—it feels so good, I drink it all day. I love jumping on my trampoline. I love getting a good night's sleep. I love sleepover parties. I love making love. I love being with a man—the touching, the caressing, the tenderness and the intimacy.

  —Jennifer Claire Moyer, actress

- Swimming with the dolphins! It's better than being a child at Disneyland.

  —Kiki Corbin, naturopathic doctor & minister

- Re-energizing in nature: a walk in the woods, skinny-dipping in a lake, getting away from anything human!

  —Wendy Read, reconciliation analyst & fabric artist

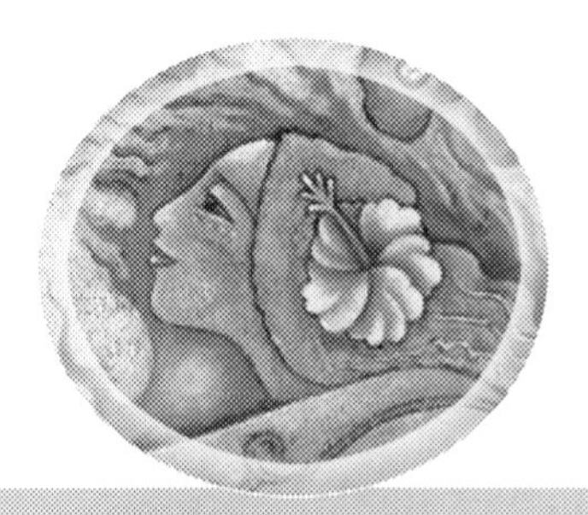

TURNING *your own* STONES

Get together with some girlfriends—in person or on-line—and ask yourselves these questions. You might want to write down the answers first, then share them with each other.

1. What boundaries do you need to set, and what boundaries do you need to break?
2. Where are you overgiving at the expense of your own well-being?
3. Where are you undergiving at the expense of your own well-being?
4. How do you create stillness for yourself, or how could you?
5. Can you think of a really juicy, full-out way to play?
6. What's your favorite way to take care of yourself?

9

Accessing Authentic Female Power

◆

Women can uniquely reconcile
the coexistence of pain and pleasure,
the spiritual and the secular, intellect
and intuition, and the tangible and
mysterious nature of the universe.

—Madeleine L'Engle, author

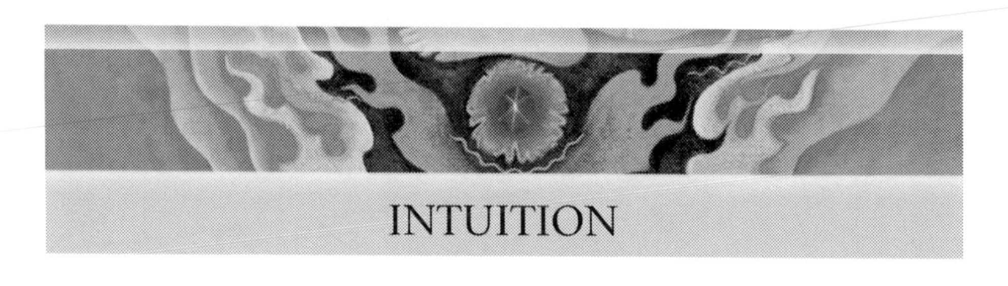

INTUITION

Honey, that's when your gut gets it
before your head gets around to figuring it out.

—NAOMI JUDD, SINGER

- I have learned several things about the intuitive process. First, intuition is persistent. You hear it in the middle of the night, at stoplights, in line at the grocery store, while talking to a friend on the phone. . . . It's a quiet sense of direction or an idea about an action to take.

  —*Carol Adrienne,* THE PURPOSE OF YOUR LIFE

- It may seem strange, but in order to be intuitive, you cannot be concerned with being right. Your very anxiety will interfere with the intuitive process. Fears, hopes and expectations have no place in intuition.

  —*Rosemary Ellen Guiley,* BREAKTHROUGH INTUITION

- Intuition and rational thinking work beautifully together if you honor both of them. Sometimes intuition may come with a bit of fear, because usually it is pushing you out of your comfort zone a little. So don't automatically assume that the fear is a "no." It may just be a signal that this is a new territory.

—*Carol Adrienne,* THE PURPOSE OF YOUR LIFE

- Your intuition is not complete until you act on it. Taking action strengthens the intuitive facility. . . . If you call the muse for help, you must honor the process in full.

  —*Rosemary Ellen Guiley,* BREAKTHROUGH INTUITION

- Because of their agelong training in human relations—for that is what feminine intuition really is—women have a special contribution to make to any group enterprise. . . .

  —*Margaret Mead, anthropologist*

When we assert intuition, we are . . . like the starry night; we gaze at the world through a thousand eyes.

—CLARISSA PINKOLA ESTÉS, *WOMEN WHO RUN WITH THE WOLVES*

OPEN HEART

It is in the tearing open of the heart that we discover how guarded our lives have become, how small a cage we have traded off for safe ground.

—STEPHEN LEVINE, POET, AUTHOR & SPIRITUAL COUNSELOR

- The secret to living more happily is keeping an open mind, a healthy curiosity and an open heart—a desire to learn and explore, no matter what the source, the subject or the circumstances. With this attitude, it doesn't matter who you're with and what you're doing—you're going to find something new.

  —Jacquelina Davis, LMT & NIA instructor

- Keeping an open heart is one of the greatest responsibilities we are challenged with. It is a moral objective to culture keeping your heart open. Anything done without that objective is superficial and even destructive.

  —Amy McCarrel, seminar leader & women's group facilitator

- Opening your heart does not equal pastel colors—it encompasses the whole range of emotions. We are all artists at avoiding what is uncomfortable.

—Jennifer Garcia, seminar leader & women's group facilitator

◆

I *believe that everyone, young and old, has the same life purpose—to live a life that gives and receives love with an open heart and a healthy body.*

—SUE HUGGINS, FULL-TIME MOTHER

SPIRITUALITY & ENLIGHTENMENT

Spiritual love is a position of standing with one hand extended into the universe and one hand extended into the world, letting ourselves be a conduit for passing energy.

—CHRISTINA BALDWIN, AUTHOR, SPEAKER & EDUCATOR

- We feel something missing. Inside of us is a void, a longing deep within for some elusive satisfaction. This empty feeling is often experienced physically as gnawing hunger, as if we have a bottomless hole inside. . . . For so many women, it's a longing for spiritual fulfillment that leaves us always hungry and dissatisfied.

  —Lynn Ginsburg & Mary Taylor, WHAT ARE YOU HUNGRY FOR?

- Spirituality is not limited to religion. Religion can lead to a greater knowing of one's spiritual nature, but true spirituality is the actual experience of the divine. Whatever nourishes your heart—rocking a baby, watching a sunset, singing, looking at a magnificent tree—these experiences, done with awareness, can connect you to the center of your being, the home of spirit.

—Elinor Hall, life skills coach

- Along the way, I have learned that enlightenment is not something you attain but rather a journey that unfolds daily as a gift of grace. Enlightenment is the growth of wisdom, the ever-increasing capacity for living the essence of love. It is not intellectual knowledge or miracles of the ego. It is a deep, mysterious and living connection with your soul.

  —Farida Sharan, FLOWER CHILD

- My experience of God is the love I feel for others. Even though this is beyond words, I access this through my thoughts, speech and actions. Every thought, intention and deed sculpts who we are and how we live. I feel closest to God when I am working with children. It is through service that we live that love.

  —Lori Schreier, attorney, mediator & facilitator

◆

How is it possible that a being with such sensitive jewels as the eyes, such enchanted musical instruments as the ears, and such a fabulous arabesque of nerves as the brain can experience itself as anything less than God?

—ALAN WATTS, AUTHOR & LECTURER

GRATITUDE

I like living. I have sometimes been wildly, despairingly, acutely miserable, racked with sorrow, but through it all I still know quite certainly that just to be alive is a grand thing.

—AGATHA CHRISTIE, ENGLISH WRITER

- Gratitude unlocks the fullness of life. It turns what we have into enough, and more. It turns denial into acceptance, chaos to order, confusion to clarity. It can turn a meal into a feast, a house into a home, a stranger into a friend. Gratitude makes sense of our past, brings peace for today, and creates a vision for tomorrow.

  —Melody Beattie, in WOMEN ON LIFE, Rosalie Maggio

- When we give gratitude—spontaneously throughout the day and intentionally before sleep—we attract more things to be grateful for. We start opening to beauty and grace and others. It's not just saying thank you; it's really feeling appreciation. Pay attention to the good—the good things, the good people, the good opportunities, the good music.

—Elinor Hall, life skills coach

- It's important to appreciate what you have when you have it, because we don't know what life will hold from day to day. You always think you have plenty of time—to say "I love you," or fix your relationship with your mother or father—but you may not.

  —Ellen Greene, classics professor

There's a self-expansive aspect of gratitude.
Very possibly it's a little known law of nature:
the more gratitude you have, the more you have to be grateful for.

—ELAINE ST. JAMES, AUTHOR

COMPASSION

If you want others to be happy, practice compassion.
If you want to be happy, practice compassion.

—DALAI LAMA, SPIRITUAL LEADER

- When compassion arises, we see we are interconnected, and we feel the pain of others as our own. We can walk in a spirit of friendship, witness, support and love. We can be allies for each other.

  —*Mirabai Bush*, COMPASSION IN CREATION

- Compassion means kindness, patience and forgiveness for myself and for others. Compassion is a lifelong lesson and challenge. The gift for me is to learn what it is to feel authentic compassion for the people in positions of power in our world, who continue the dance of separation, domination, control, fear . . . this is how to become part of the solution.

  —*Candace Freeland, photographer, musician & peace activist*

- As a helping professional, I feel that compassion is the balance between an open heart and a quiet mind. Without overidentifying or resisting the suffering of another, one can be most effective. That place of balance is critical in avoiding the burnout so common in the helping professions.

  Diane Haug, psychotherapist

- For me, compassion is when the moment silences me, and I am suddenly aware that I am not separate from anyone or anything. I feel moved beyond belief by the incredible grace that connects all. Gratitude overflows.

  —Bren Frisch, graphic artist & mom

- On a tangible, everyday level, it means that in every moment in every situation you are able to ask yourself, *What is the most loving thing I can do right now?*

  —Kiki Corbin, naturopathic doctor & minister

◆

Compassion is not something you do. It's a feeling that arises when there's the deepest realization that this river of life that flows through me is the same river of life that flows through everybody and everything that exists.

—JENNIFER CLAIRE MOYER, ACTRESS

ACCOUNTABILITY

Take your life in your own hands, and what happens?
A terrible thing: no one to blame.

—ERICA JONG, AMERICAN WRITER & FEMINIST

- One of the most powerful tools in business, when the situation occurs, is to freely accept responsibility and avoid blaming. I've seen many volatile situations be diffused when I acknowledged that a problem had occurred, and that I would take responsibility for it and ensure that it got corrected. Inevitably, these situations resulted in my gaining more power within the structure rather than being weakened.

  —Linda Elliott, former executive vice president, Visa

- Accountability is a powerful side of growth. It is the other side of blame. When we are able to examine our lives with compassion and a measure of emotional detachment, we are often able to see that we give away our freedom when we point blame towards another for our experience. So much chaos and destruction come from not wanting to be accountable for our own emotions and actions in this world. Personal transformation and growth arise from taking responsibility for every choice and aspect of our lives.

—Andrea Girman, women's health practitioner & pediatrician

- I had to give up guilt, give up blame, and know that when it's all said and done that I am the person responsible for my own self. Not a husband or a manager or even my child. Just me—and the Lord, of course.

  —Loretta Lynn, I'M STILL WOMAN ENOUGH

◆

Accountability is what happens when our words and deeds become congruent.

—MELISSA MICHAELS, EDUCATOR, SOCIAL ARTIST & MOTHER

HONESTY

Honesty is not something to flirt with. We must be married to it.

—ANONYMOUS

- You never find yourself until you face the truth.

  —Pearl Bailey, singer & actress

- I never had secrets from my children. I was always honest about my struggles and my faults, bringing the dark part of my life into the light. Telling the truth is what creates intimacy and freedom.

  —Farida Sharan, natural physician

- I don't need a mirror to see how I look. Long ago, I realized the inner self is visible if you present yourself truthfully and authentically.

  —Geraldine Smith in WISE WOMEN, Joyce Tennyson

- Honesty is a two-edged sword, and it takes great strength to wield this power tool. Perhaps that is why it is not used more often. Honesty has helped many a leader gain prestige, trust and position. On the other hand, honesty is also the reason why many people end up "second in command" and never at the top. So the question becomes, are you strong enough to accept second place, but know that you can live completely with your words and actions?

  —Linda Elliott, former vice president, Visa

◆

We kid ourselves into thinking that a little white lie won't matter. And it does. It hurts us. Dishonesty is expensive. It erodes the soul.

—ANNE WILSON SCHAEF, *NATIVE WISDOM FOR WHITE MINDS*

When I was working on Wall Street many years ago, I loved my job, and I found that the man I was working for was being dishonest. He wanted me to type something, and when I refused, I was fired. I loved this job, but it wasn't worth giving up my integrity. Once I had typed it, it would have been my lie, too. Incidentally, he later got fired and I got hired back.

—Wanda Roth, fashion & jewelry consultant

FORGIVENESS

To forgive is to set a prisoner free and discover the prisoner was you.

—UNKNOWN

- Life is too short not to love and forgive everyone. When you hold a grudge, your body is in contraction. You live in sadness, and lose the focus of the loving being you are naturally. In allowing love and forgiveness, you reclaim your true nature, which is love.

  —Carol Richter, spiritual counselor

- Forgiveness is the most important thing. We all have to forgive what was done to us—the Irish people have to forgive, the African people, the Jewish people—all have to forgive and understand. The only way to stop the cycle of hate and abuse is not to allow yourself to get caught up in it.

  —Sinead O'Connor, singer & songwriter

- We are so inextricably linked to our mothers and hold them in the cells of our bodies. No matter what the pain has been, we need to forgive. Our mothers feel the same pain we do, and the more we forgive, the more that pain is liberated for your mother and yourself.

  —*Maya Charney, academic counselor*

- Forgiveness is a key part of surrender and when you express gratitude it is the highest form of forgiveness. Find the kindness, the gift and the freedom disguised in the things which are hard to forgive. It's not easy to let some things go, but it's harder on you to stay hard.

  —*Lori Schreier, attorney, mediator & facilitator*

- In *A Course in Miracles* we learn: "You are never upset for the reason you think." Therefore don't blame your partners and become angry with them. What they did probably stirred up in you the memory of something similar for which you have not forgiven someone.

  —*Sondra Ray, LOVING RELATIONSHIPS*

Forgiveness is the act of admitting we are like other people.

—CHRISTINA BALDWIN, AUTHOR, SPEAKER & EDUCATOR

SURRENDER & TRUST

When you come to the edge of all the light you know, and are about to step off into the darkness of the unknown, faith is knowing one of two things will happen. There will be something solid to stand on, or you will be taught how to fly.

—BARBARA J. WINTER, ENTREPRENEUR, WRITER & SPEAKER

- Surrender is giving up control but not losing power.

  —Sondra Ray, author

- You are supposed to be here. Each one of us is part of a chromatic scale, a musical note without which the symphony would be incomplete and orchestration would be impossible. When you can surrender to this and allow your note to be fulfilled as you, trusting your own unique tone, the struggle ends and the music begins.

  —Vickie Jimenz, financial analyst & healer

- One of the primary differences between men and women is that women have a cellular experience of surrender. Not surrender in a victim sense, but for women, there's always something going on for us that's bigger than us: our periods, or having children, or going through menopause . . . being a part of the rhythm of the universe and having no choice but going with it.

  —Beth VanArsdale Krier, divorce attorney

- The greatest revelation I've had is to learn to live without knowing, and have that be okay. I could not have written a five-year plan for my life and have it turn out the way it has, because it is so much vaster than anything I could have imagined. Sometimes it's just okay not to know.

  —Arielle Ford, media relations expert & author

◆

We journey blind on our way back to family, to faith, to God, as we understand Him. But the blindness is a requisite part of process. We can no longer control; we have to trust.

—BETTY FORD, AMERICAN FIRST LADY

SERVICE

After the verb "To Love" . . . "To Help"
is the most beautiful verb in the world.

—BERTHA VON SUTTNER, AUSTRIAN PACIFIST
& FIRST WOMAN RECIPIENT OF THE NOBEL PEACE PRIZE

- Some people give time, some money, some their skills and connections, some literally give their life's blood . . . but everyone has something to give.

  —Barbara Bush, American First Lady

- Anybody who feels they're stuck in self-criticism, get out there and take care of your fellow people. You'll find who you really are in the reflection of their love and their smiles and their appreciation and their joy in you.

  —Shane Orne, riding coach & mother

- I've worked with the homeless as case manager and food service manager. It made me so grateful for what I have and allowed me to recognize the simple humanity that exists in us all. Those I served gave me more by far than I gave them. Being able to make a difference just by sharing your heart and being human, taking time with others, asking them about their lives, just being there—for me this cultured a great deal of compassion and sense of purpose.

—Jenn Holden, social worker

- When I ask myself the question, "Why am I here?" the picture of just living my little life and passing on seems reasonable enough, yet, somehow incomplete. Remember the phrase, "If you're not part of the solution, you're part of the problem"? Take it on. You've got a job to do as a key player in making the world a better place. It's a labor of love. There is no higher work.

—Valerie Stricklett, sculptor & human services administrator

◆

Great opportunities to help others seldom come,
but small ones surround us daily.

—SALLY KOCH, AUTHOR

LEADERSHIP & POWER

To work in the world lovingly means that we are defining what we will be for, rather than reacting to what we are against.

—CHRISTINA BALDWIN, AUTHOR, SPEAKER & EDUCATOR

- It is imperative that we look to the feminine principle for the collective healing so desperately needed in these times. Women's leadership looks different. Authentic female power includes trusting our heart and emotional life and bringing qualities like empathy, intuition and receptivity into the way we work.

  —Diane Haug, psychotherapist

- Power is a great word if you understand what real power is. It's not getting what you want or manipulating others. I see power as being more akin to wisdom. For women, it's easier for their higher self to be connected with their minds and hearts, and that's true power, that's where true wisdom comes from.

  —Kiki Corbin, naturopathic doctor & minister

- Women have for centuries been recognized as talented listeners, nurturers, motivators, excellent communicators. These very qualities that we once were told were unbusinesslike are precisely the qualities that business needs most to tap human potential.

  —Mary Cunningham Agee, entrepreneur & author

- It's amazing how fast doors open to us when we dare to take control of a situation.

  —Catherine Ponder, author

- It's better to be a lion for a day than a sheep all your life.

  —Sister Elizabeth Kenny, nurse, pioneer in the treatment of polio

◆

Leadership is not a formula or a program, it is a human activity that comes from the heart and considers the hearts of others.

—LANCE SECRETAN, *INDUSTRY WEEK*

INTENTION

A good intention clothes itself with sudden power.

—RALPH WALDO EMERSON, AUTHOR, PHILOSOPHER & POET

- I have spent long hours pondering my work in the world, trying to decide what to do with my life that will make the greatest contribution. And each time I go to the Grandmothers, the elders who have been my teachers for so many years . . . their gentle but adamant response is always the same: "It doesn't matter, Oriah. It doesn't matter *what* you do. What matters is *how* you do whatever you choose to do."

  —Oriah Mountain Dreamer, author & poet

- I have never placed restrictions around what I have wanted. There is nothing in my life that I have really wanted that I haven't gotten. It's not luck—it's having a clear intention and the confidence that there isn't anything that can't be overcome. I'm not afraid to do whatever it takes to make it happen.

  —Alexis Mayne, president, natural cosmetics company

- If you can't do it with love and cheerfulness, don't do it at all—go home.

—Mother Teresa, humanitarian

◆

Intention is ten thousand times more real and strong than what we consider physical reality.

—J & B

COMMITMENT

Diamonds are only chunks of coal that stuck to their jobs, you see.

—MINNIE RICHARD SMITH, POET

- I can honestly say that I was never affected by the question of the success of an undertaking. If I felt it was the right thing to do, I was for it regardless of the possible outcome.

  —Golda Meir, Israeli prime minister

- Hope begins in the dark, the stubborn hope that if you just show up and try to do the right thing, the dawn will come. You wait and watch and work: You don't give up.

  —Anne Lamott, author

- Discipline is an act of love. When you care enough about something to be consistent with it over time, whether it's dance, a child, a community . . . that dedicated, consistent attention allows the possible to become manifest.

  —Melissa Michaels, educator, social artist & mother

- You may have to fight a battle more than once to win it.

  —Margaret Thatcher, former British prime minister

- I used to want the words "She tried" on my tombstone. Now I want "She did it."

  —Katherine Dunham, dancer & choreographer

♦

Committing to what is right, what is just, and what is good will bring you fulfillment.

—CORETTA SCOTT KING, IN *WISE WOMEN,* JOYCE TENNYSON

LIVING *in the* PRESENT

Don't tell me how wonderful things will be . . . some day.
Show me that you can risk being completely at peace,
truly okay with the way things are right
now in this moment, and again in the next and next.

—ORIAH MOUNTAIN DREAMER, *THE DANCE*

- Take one day at a time, one hour, one minute. To live in the future is impossible and invites trouble; to live in the past is impossible and invites regret.

  —Elinor Hall, life skills coach

- More and more my life practice is simply to be with what is, to accept the things the way they are and to open my heart today. I realize that if I cannot be happy and embrace today, when will I? Don't postpone your joy.

  —Sue Berkey, yoga teacher & mother

- Don't spend your time regretting anything. Live the best you can every day. And if at some point there's something from the past you regret, just come right back to the moment and say, "This is what's happening now."

  —*Sue Huggins, full-time mother*

- If I do one thing at a time, really focus on that, totally take it in and enjoy it and don't feel as if I have to get on to the next thing, then there's joy in everything I do and in moving between things, too.

  —*DH, business & family manager*

- . . . The thing is that you don't know if you're going to live long enough to slow down, relax, and have fun, and discover the truth of your spiritual identity. You may not be destined to live a long life; you may not have sixty more years to discover and claim your own deepest truth—like Breaker Morant said, "You have to live every day as if it's your last, because one of these days, you're bound to be right."

  —*Anne Lamott, author, Berkeley graduation talk, May 2003*

Eternity is not something that begins after you are dead.
It is going on all the time. We are in it now.

—CHARLOTTE PERKINS GILMAN, AMERICAN WRITER

Following the breakup of my first marriage, I was living an extreme life in all ways. I could not figure out what was going to happen down the road. I could only see what the next step was. I had a sign on my refrigerator that said: "Just make lunch." It was training for living in the moment. There's no knowing what the crystal ball holds, but every outcome starts with "making lunch."

—Stacy Hurlin, artist & community leader

EMBRACING LIFE

I feel very adventurous. There are so many doors to be opened, and I'm not afraid to look behind them.

—ELIZABETH TAYLOR, ACTRESS

- So many opportunities are open to women now, and now is the time to surge forward, to embrace all that is open to us. We also want to forge paths to those opportunities that still elude us. We always have a choice in everything we do. We decide, we act, we succeed and we enjoy—or not! Do whatever makes you happy.

  —Maggie Argiro, writer

- I have never felt that there is a positive purpose to pretending that all is well when it is not. I believe that the depths and the heights of life are equally valuable in creating an authentic, fully integrated human being. If you know someone that you think has a perfect existence, think again. We all experience challenges, anguish, longing, laughter and joy.

  —Farida Sharan, FLOWER CHILD

- Trying to get to a place of perfection or even just "okayness" and fixating on that goal is a classic way of running away from yourself, of avoiding who you are. The journey begins with exactly where you are, how you are and who you are. Embracing your life now is the goal.

—Barbara Foster, artist & Vedic astrologer

◆

Living never wore one out so much as the effort not to live.

—ANAÏS NIN, AMERICAN (FRENCH-BORN) AUTHOR

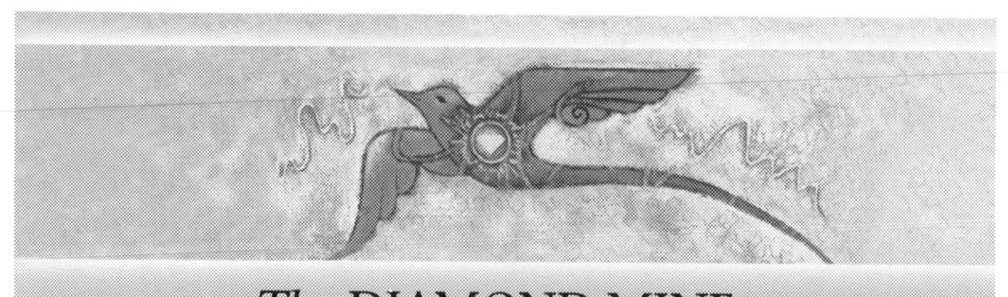

The DIAMOND MINE:
What do you love about being a woman?

- I love being able to wear all the colors without feeling weird. I love belly dancing and moving my body. I love smelling and wearing scents and essential oils. I love that we are naturally nurturers and mothers, and that we put relationships before business. This is what the world needs more of now. I love that we know how to fluidly connect socially and be intimate with each other.

  —Lori Schreier, attorney, mediator & facilitator

- I think I love everything about my right brain, and that it's so easy to access. I love my emotional body, that I have a much bigger menu of emotions than most of the males I know. It makes life so rich. I love that I'm nonlinear. I especially love my opportunity to be a mother. I've lived two lives, one before my child and one after. Motherhood has enlightened me, because I've never felt the level of love that I have when I look at my child.

  —Holly Moore, artist & mother

- Being a woman, I feel the power to experience nature, to be nature, to know nature, to know my nature, to create out of the force of Mother Nature anything that I desire for my life and for the good of others and the planet. I feel I'm very close to that primordial power of creation being a woman.

  —Lilli Botchis, alchemical researcher & adviser

- Being a woman is just the cards I was dealt in this life So far it has been a fascinating journey of continuous discovery. Sometimes it has me grappling with great challenges; other times it's pure delight. However, the most important thing for me is to reach the state of life where I am saturated with the essence of all things—pure cosmic energy—and transcend the realm of any gender.

  —Emilie Taylor, wife, mother & strategic planner

- When I feel a sense of ease and enjoyment, I really set the tempo for the rest of the family. I love that sense of flow that would be absent if I weren't there. It's juicy. It's just enjoying and savoring what's going on, as opposed to making sure what's going on is right.

  —Sue Huggins, full-time mother

- I love my body. I love its curves and its softness and its smoothness. I love having babies, taking care of them and raising them up to be wonderful, big people. And I love having a partner to make choices with.

  —DH, business & family manager

- I love the curves, circles, roundness; everything ovular visually and internally. Being part of the squiggle and not the straight line.

  —Valerie Stricklett, sculptor & human services administrator

- I love the ever-changing seasons of my emotions, and the wisdom they offer. I love the depth to which I can feel my grief, my joy, my anger, my love. I love how freely tears flow—of sorrow, beauty, longing or delight—and how they cleanse and renew my soul. I love the strength of my softness and the power of my grace. I love my connection to the moon, which connects me to every other woman on the earth. And I love getting dressed up, adorning and anointing and celebrating the uniquely beautiful woman that is me today!

  —Morgan Lazzaro-Smith, youth mentor

- I like the way we can have a diffuse way of looking at everything, that we can see it, feel it, hear it, touch it all simultaneously. Guys can get things done, but can they simultaneously know what's cooking in the kitchen, listen to the music, talk to their best friend and send an e-mail at the same time?

  —Arielle Ford, media relations expert & author

STEPPING-STONES
for ACCESSING AUTHENTIC FEMALE POWER

- Keep a journal. Be sure to include experiences in which you feel connected to the divine or times when you feel totally present, enormously big and expanded.

  —Elinor Hall, life skills coach

- One of the secrets of a long and fruitful life is to forgive everybody everything every night before you go to bed.

  —Anonymous

- When I can use my voice as an instrument of my heart, then power just courses through my body head to foot. When I can dance and stomp my feet and move my body in ways that my body needs to move, then I'm in a space of freedom and power, limitless. When I can drum, the grace of the great mystery is with me and the group, and I am more in my power than I ever have been.

—Candace Freeland, photographer, musician & peace activist

- I recently created a new ritual. On some Saturdays when I can, I go into silence for six hours. I won't have a plan. I might go for a walk, I'll do my meditation, maybe guided visualization, journal, color—no TV or anything outer directed. Sometimes I'll look through old photo albums or journals, or just look out the window—just be. The first time I did it, it was so profoundly relaxing. It was a deep, deep rest inside my soul.

  —Arielle Ford, media relations expert & author

- I find that when I'm resisting a difficult, painful, confusing experience and when I complain and bitch, the most powerful tool for trust and surrender is to write down everything I am grateful for, even the very thing that is causing the pain. This is an antidote to fear, resentment, depression, resistance and negativity.

  —Lori Schreier, attorney, mediator & facilitator

- Gratitude has been one of the most significant tools I've consciously used to bring more grace and more good into my life. When I was at the lowest point in my life, I started practicing gratitude every day by spending five minutes at the end of my day focusing on what I was grateful for. That was the thing that shifted my life more than anything during that time.

  —Marci Shimoff, professional speaker & coauthor

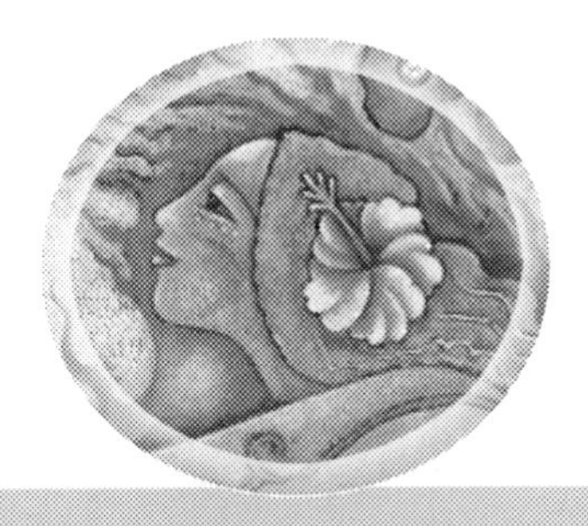

TURNING *your own* STONES

Get together with some girlfriends—in person or on-line—and ask yourselves these questions. You might want to write down the answers first, then share them with each other.

1. Make a journal that you use only for intuitive insights and begin following the trail of those hunches to completion, noting when you acted or didn't.
2. What does "spirituality" mean to you, and how do you live that in your day?
3. What are you grateful for right now in your life?
4. What and who is left for you to forgive?
5. What do you love about being a woman?

10

The Overflowing Jewel Box

◆

You were once wild here.
Don't let them tame you!

—Isadora Duncan, American dancer

Is There Anything More You'd Like to Offer Young Women?

- My best advice in life is: Don't waste any time feeling guilty. See the job, do the job, stay out of the misery. Try to put yourself in the other person's shoes. Love is the only thing worth accumulating. Cultivate a personal relationship with God because that's what will interest you most as life goes on. Take good care of your body—it has a great deal to do with how happy you are. Make a habit of looking within for answers, not without. Surround yourself with good company and people of all ages.

  —Sheila Ross, mother, wife & community leader

- I'm a big believer in taking one day at a time. I haven't always done that. I don't play "What if?" I've learned since I had cancer that every day counts—I realize how precious life is. I try to do something for others every day, even if it's just a smile. And I try to do something for myself every day, try to enjoy myself every day.

  —Maureen Read, seniors tennis player

- I have had to stop thinking, "Well, I would have felt good *if* I'd gotten enough sleep. I would have felt good *if* I'd eaten the right food." I've had to just think, "Well, I didn't, and I probably won't tomorrow or the next day or the next day either." I have to say, "This is now. I have a great life that millions of people would give anything to have. Start enjoying it. Enjoy it tired." Learning how to live through that edge and stay blissful has been one of the most soul-forming parts of my life.

  —*Sue Huggins, full-time mother*

- Take it slow. Once the flower is picked, it can't be returned to the vine. You have enough time to unfold. The apple will naturally fall. Let yourself have that. There is power that comes from gathering all the nutrients from the earth and the tree from which you come. Then become your own fruit.

  —*Melissa Michaels, educator, social artist & mother*

- No matter how turbulent it is on the outside, in spite of the burdens or the boredom or the challenges in life, there is a calm and peace inside that we can seek and find. I call it bliss, and it is our true nature, the only part of us that's real.

  —*B. Mawiyah Clayborne, How to Remember Your Bliss*

- It is an amazing gift to be born a female at this time on earth. It takes tremendous courage, dedication and love to be here now. As women, we carry the sacredness of life, we uphold the light and protect it. We have an internal compass that is unfailing. No matter what has been beaten into us regarding the status of women, always know that you have the power to change the world, to heal the planet and to further our evolution in a positive direction.

—Indigo Margolis, minister, counselor & poet

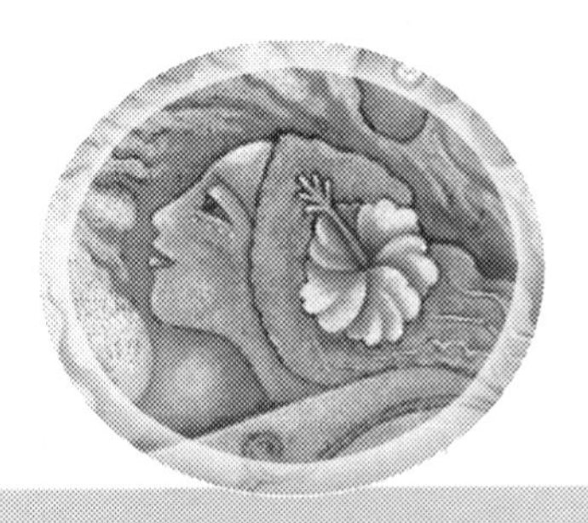

TURNING *your own* STONES

What are some of the most important things you've already learned in your life, and what would you offer to other young women to inspire their lives?

ABOUT *the* AUTHORS & ARTIST

Jennifer Read Hawthorne is coauthor of the #1 *New York Times* best seller, *Chicken Soup for the Woman's Soul,* and the #1 *New York Times* and #1 *USA Today* best seller *Chicken Soup for the Mother's Soul*. She is an inspirational speaker who delivers keynote addresses internationally.

Barbara Warren Holden has been married to her partner, Paul, for twenty years and has a fifteen-year-old son, Bryan. She is a Montessori teacher, with degrees in art and literature. She has studied yoga for over twenty-five years and has facilitated women's groups. She is currently teaching yoga in Colorado.

Mara Friedman is the artist whose image *Sunrise Ruby* was used in the design of the cover and throughout this book. To receive a catalog of Mara's work, please contact her at New Moon Visions, P. O. Box 23, Lorane, OR 97451, or telephone her at 541-942-9057, or explore her Web site at *http://www.newmoonvisions.com.*